LEARNING TO WORSHIP

THEODOR FILTHAUT

LEARNING
TO
WORSHIP

Translated by
RONALD WALLS

CHALLONER BOOKS

LONDON: BURNS & OATES

Originally published in German
by Patmos Verlag, Düsseldorf

Translation © 1965 by
BURNS & OATES LTD.

Catalogue No. 5/5736

SET IN GREAT BRITAIN BY GEORGE BERRIDGE AND CO. LTD.
STEWARD STREET, LONDON, E.I. AND PRINTED BY
FLETCHER AND SON LTD. NORWICH, FOR
BURNS AND OATES LTD. 25 ASHLEY PLACE LONDON, S.W.I

CONTENTS

PREFACE

This book is not a liturgical treatise – either in the specialist or in the popular sense – but seeks rather to tackle some of the educational tasks presented by the liturgical revival.

At the centre of this investigation stands man, who celebrates the public worship of the Church. Our question concerns the equipment of the man who is not merely an onlooker at, but a bearer of, worship, and whose whole life stands in meaningful relationship to this act of worship. Hence we take leave of catechetical instruction in the narrower sense. Because we are dealing with nothing less than man himself, we must strike at once deeper and over a wider field. Nonetheless the catechetical aspect will not be neglected as a result of this anthropological aim. On the contrary it will receive a more solid foundation and at the same time be integrated within the whole process of education.

Because this book is addressed to teachers as well as to priests, technical theological terms have been avoided as far as possible. It is true that, in contrast to the vague and elusive language common in catechetical writing, great importance is attached to precise concepts which make no attempt to deny their theological and philosophical ancestry. On the other hand, the clarity sought in this way ought not to be achieved at the expense of liveliness.

I

HISTORY'S ANSWER TO SOME QUESTIONS

*The significance and limitation of an
historical consideration of our problem*

OUR theme: basic problems of liturgical education, directs our attention to the present day.
We are concerned with the situation and the
tasks facing liturgical education *today*. We seek light
on some of the basic questions affecting our practical
life. Such an examination of the present can easily
lead to one-sided and exaggerated assessments, judge-
ments and demands. The best antidote to this is
provided by an historical study; and in the liturgy we
are in fact dealing with an historical entity. In respect
of its forms, the liturgy is predominantly a product
of historical development. During the course of almost two thousand years of the history of Christian
worship there have been times of blossoming and
times of decay. We may take it for granted that all
ages have applied themselves to the problems of
liturgical instruction and education, some with great
vigour, some perhaps with less. It is bound to help us
in our enquiry if we glance at the most important
periods of liturgical education and determine what
predicament in public worship was being faced from

1

time to time, and how men have set about solving
the problems presented to them. To disprove the sort
of idea that it is only now that men are beginning to
do something about the liturgy, we need go no further
than German history. Not only the period of the
Enlightenment and the following Romantic period,
but the sixteenth century, even, was characterized by
wide-spread and lively interest in pastoral liturgy.
We may suppose, therefore, that it will be worth
while finding out which problems of liturgical education were acute in these and in other periods. It is
by no means a waste of time to raise the question
whether perhaps the contemporary situation in public
worship is not so utterly new and unique in the
history of the Church after all, and whether we are
not – in this as in many other things – caught up in
the great context of history. An historical enquiry,
then, can exercise a significant and helpful function.
True, it has to be an enquiry carried out with an eye
upon the present; but, on the other hand, that does
not mean that we are to project our contemporary
problems into past history. Were we to proceed in
that fashion we should be cheated of the real contri-
bution which history has to offer to the present day.
We are utterly intent on discovering what was and
what it was like; but we are not disinterested en-
quirers. We are interested in knowing just what the
situation really was. It is as living men that we
interrogate history, as men, caught up in the mighty
stream of history, but called at the same time by
their power of decision to help to determine the future

course of that stream. Because we must write not a history of liturgical education but only a brief sketch, we are absolved from the demand of completeness. From the inescapably large number of problems which the tide of history has washed up on the shore of literary record we shall pick up this or that which we think worth while taking account of and examining.

The early centuries: liturgical education through intelligent assistance at public worship

How hard it often is to lead the faithful into the meaning of the liturgical celebrations. What a labour it is, for example, to explain the basic shape of the Mass to children or to acquaint them with the shape of the separate parts. It is no easy task to explain the meaning and form of the Canon of the Mass, shall we say, to children or even to adults, and to train them to take part in it. Frequently the forms of the liturgical celebrations turn out to be no longer immediately intelligible to men today. By contrast, for the faithful in early centuries immediate understanding of public worship was the rule. Sharing in the mysteries of public worship, people at the same time, by looking, listening, and acting, understood what they meant. Let us take the Eucharist as an example. In chapter 67 of his *Apology*, Justin, the philosopher and martyr, describes the Eucharist as it was celebrated in his own time, that is in the middle of the second century. The text is famous and much quoted – with justification. "And in the so-called day of the Sun there is a meeting of all of us who live in cities or the country, and the memoirs of the Apostles or the writings of the Prophets are read, as long as time allows. Then when the reader has ceased, the president gives by word of mouth his admonition and exhortation to follow these excellent things. Afterwards we all rise at once and offer prayers; and as I said, when we have ceased to pray, bread is brought and wine and water, and the president likewise offers up prayers and thanksgivings to the best of his power, and the people responds with its Amen. Then follows the distribution to each and the partaking of that for which thanks were given; and to them that are absent a portion is sent by the hand of the deacons."[1]

We note how this simple account, with its omissions by reason of the rule of secrecy, makes the essential structure of the Eucharist perfectly clear. It tells of the lessons, the sermon, the prayers, of the presenting of bread and wine and water, of the Eucharistic prayer over the gifts, and of their distribution. Only those things which today still make up the essential shape of the Mass are present: (1) the liturgy of the Word comprising preaching and prayers; (2) the Eucharistic liturgy comprising the preparation of the gifts, the Eucharistic prayer, and the distribution.

[1] As in Gwatkin: *Selections from Early Christian Writers* (1958) 55.

It is a transparent structure, a celebration full of meaning as a whole and in all its parts. More than the rest of the sacraments the Eucharist is characterized by the corporate nature of its celebration. For all its brevity and sketchiness the account emphasizes this factor. At the very beginning the Eucharist is called the "assembling of everybody". The lessons are not read silently by the celebrant. They are not read by him at all; he listens along with the whole congregation to the reader or lector. The prayers are described as community prayers; and it is even expressly remarked of the Eucharistic prayer that the people have to say their Amen, their word of assent. All present share in the meal. Bread and wine are distributed to all. We cannot fail to see that the structure of this celebration is that of a community, cultic meal prefaced by instruction.

And if over and above this we picture the place and the manner of the celebration, the impression is deepened that here we have an action which is immediately comprehensible to all the participants. The place we must imagine to be probably the larger room in a private house. The participants are grouped round a table or facing it. Everyone can with ease see and hear and follow all that is happening. The reader does not stand just anywhere – behind the people, for example, as is unfortunately often the practice today – but in front of the congregation and facing them. When he is reading it is taken for granted that all, the president included, listen to him. The gifts – bread and wine – are recognizably what they are without explanation. It is real bread that is laid upon the table, and this bread is broken so that all can eat of it as people do in their own homes. The community factor reaches its peak in the common eating and drinking. In these early days of the Church onlookers at Mass were the exception. Those who came took part in everything including the meal.

From Justin's text which we have taken as example we draw the conclusion that the faithful in these early days required no liturgical education in order to be able to grasp the form of a liturgical celebration. Because in the celebration the essential structures stood out in clear relief, people perceived immediately, without reflection, the whole meaning of what was taking place. For example when the reader turned towards the people and read from holy Scripture it would have been quite superfluous to explain to the audience what this man was now doing. Until recently, however, when the priest read the Epistle and the Gospel with his back to the congregation none was able to infer from this visible and more or less audible proceeding that something was in fact being read *out*. In the early Church, on the other hand, participation in public worship was of itself an instruction and a moulding of the faithful. It is true that instruction was necessary, but not instruction about the visible actions. The instruction consisted of a discourse about the invisible workings of God's grace in the holy mysteries, and an exhortation to take part properly in, and to live by, those mysteries. This instruction was usually associated with the sacramental celebrations. It was given with particular intensity before or after Baptism. An excellent and beautiful example of this sort of liturgical instruction is provided by the mystical catecheses attributed to Bishop Cyril of Jerusalem and presumably conducted in Jerusalem in the middle of the fourth century. This mystical instruction was obviously the most effective kind, being linked with experience and action and hence embedded in the celebration of the liturgy.

As with the form of the sacramental celebrations, so there are problems of liturgical education which are concerned with symbols and symbolic actions. The Church's public worship is full of these. Most of them come down from ancient times. Many are strange to us today and can be understood only with difficulty; many even repel us. What a heap of instruction is required before these symbols and symbolic actions can be properly grasped. Again by contrast, these things presented no problems at all to men of olden times. They were to some extent familiar with the symbolic actions of the Christian liturgy from their civic life, and these things were directly intelligible to them. Thus they did not need to be told why the priest was kissing the altar, for they did this at home. In ancient times it was the custom in many places to kiss the table before a meal; and it was a custom in worship to kiss the threshold of the temple, the statue of a god, and the altar. And so it was quite natural to kiss the table, in this case the Lord's table, during public worship, before partaking of the Eucharistic meal. Indeed, on this occasion the symbolic action acquired a more profound meaning.[2]

We could multiply examples indefinitely. More important, however, than the question about the origin of the separate symbols used in church is the fact that in general people in the ancient world stood in a living relationship to the whole world of symbols. It was in their nature to think and feel that invisible realities were seen and experienced through visible actions and material things.

Again we reach the conclusion: in the early Church liturgical education was carried out by a direct method, that is through participation in public worship. Another factor contributed. The people of those early days were educated not only by the unambiguous shape of the celebration of public worship and the immediately intelligible symbolic objects and actions, but by preaching as well. The preachers of that era were still living and thinking within the mighty conspectus of the whole divine work of redemption which bore a living relationship to the Church's worship. Their sermons were born of faith's perception of the unity of the whole story of redemption. Preaching assumed an important place in public worship not in a merely external way, but became inspired through its living connection with the liturgical action. Hence the type of sermon itself encour-

[2] Cf. J. A. Jungmann, S.J.: *Public Worship* (1960) 15; and *The Mass of the Roman Rite* (1959) 210 f.

aged the faithful to adopt the right attitude to the liturgy. The supreme examples of this sort of preaching are the discourses of St. Augustine (354-430) and those of Pope St. Leo I (d. 461).

We must mention one last factor which made the liturgical education of the faithful easy. In this respect too our situation today differs from that of the early Church. This is the factor of language. In the early days there was no language problem in the liturgy. Since the days of the apostles the unquestioned practice had been to celebrate public worship in the language understood by all present. There was no so-called liturgical language understood only by the liturgical ministers. Not only the lessons and sermon but the entire liturgy was conducted in the vernacular. As a result, all of the lessons, prayers, and hymns were understood at once; and consequently, much explanation that is now assumed to be necessary was superfluous. In addition, the people of those days met with many of the images, parables, and illustrations used in the liturgical texts – mostly taken from the holy Scriptures – in their every-day life. Certainly they were not totally unfamiliar with them, whereas we on the contrary require much explanation about these things as well.

We shall sum up our observations on a few of the real problems of liturgical education in early Christian times by making use of a set of ideas taken from modern pedagogics. Modern educational science makes the distinction between intentional and functional education. One man can be educated as a result of the conscious and purposeful activity of another man. He can also be moulded by his environment which acts upon him in a variety of ways without having any such purpose in view. In the first case we speak of intentional, in the second of functional, education. The efficacy of intentional education has been and is frequently over-estimated. On the other side there is today a growing appreciation of the formative power of functional education. A well-appointed class-room exercises a formative influence upon the pupils. If it is clean and tidy, has bright, cheerful colours and good wall decoration, it produces an effect. The room acts through its very existence and moulds the children. Similarly a bad, dirty, uncared for room exerts a pernicious influence. The milieu acts in the same way. It is in the place of worship, however, that functional education reaches the height of its efficacy.

Applying these educational categories to the liturgy of the early Church, we can sum up as follows: the liturgical education of the faithful followed the functional rather than the intentional pattern. The correct attitude was aroused by the arrangement of the place of worship with a view to the performance of the liturgical celebration, and by the public worship, intelligently experienced and actively shared. The intentional form of liturgical education supplied by sermon or instruction was most effective for the very reason that it took place within the framework of public worship, so that what was said never remained in the realm of sheer abstract idea, but could be seen, experienced, and performed.[3]

The Middle Ages:
allegory governs liturgical instruction

The most important questions of liturgical education by far concern the Eucharist, the form of its celebration, and instruction about it.

The *De officiis ecclesiasticis* of Archbishop Isidore of Seville (d. 636) marked a decisive change in liturgical preaching and instruction, a change fraught with momentous consequences. This work contains, amongst other things, a commentary on the Mass which synthesizes all previous thought, but at the same time directs it into fresh channels.[4]

In the early centuries the Mass was regarded principally as the Church's great sacrifice of praise and thanksgiving, as the *Eucharist*. Hence that age was aware of the supreme and central significance of the Eucharistic prayer of consecration. Now this is changed. In his commentary Isidore of Seville separates the Preface from the Canon. The Preface now becomes nothing more than an introduction to the

---

[3] Cf. *Constitution on the Sacred Liturgy* of the Second Vatican Council (hereafter abbreviated as *Const.*), art. 1 on the aims of liturgical reform; and arts. 47-56 on reform of the Mass.

[4] Cf. F. X. Arnold: *Vorgeschichte und Einfluss des Trienter Messopferdekrets auf die Behandlung des eucharistischen Geheimnisses in der Glaubensverkündigung der Neuzeit.* (In F. X. Arnold—B. Fischer: *Die Messe in der Glaubensverkündigung*, Freiburg[2] 1953, 123-9).

Canon. Hitherto the Preface and the whole Canon had formed a single great prayer of thanksgiving in the course of which the Consecration took place. Now the prayer of thanksgiving (i.e. the Preface) and the words of consecration become separated. The Canon alone is regarded as the prayer through which the Consecration is effected. As a result the sense of a connection between Eucharist and Consecration is lost. Something else results as well. Not only does the idea that the Mass is the great sacrifice of praise and thanksgiving fall into the background, but the fact that the Mass is a sacrifice made by the Church also, loses its power. In place of this, another idea comes to the fore. The fact that in the Mass Christ becomes present in his passion, his sacrifice, his body and blood, now becomes the dominant thought. From this time onwards the problem of the Consecration, too, becomes a question of some interest. This does not mean that in the early centuries these truths had not been known and believed. They were indeed well known. And again on the other hand the truths about the Mass being the Church's sacrifice of thanksgiving did not completely fade from the Church's consciousness in the later period. We are not speaking of an *either or*, but of a shift of emphasis. These very shifts of emphasis, however, became momentous for liturgical education. The practical expositions of the Mass propagated in the Middle Ages amongst clergy and laity are all rooted in this change in the theological doctrine of the Mass. These see the Mass as the symbolic representation of the historical life and passion of Christ. It is now allegory, with its love of symbols and acting, which takes control of expositions of the Mass. Each part of the Mass – so it was thought and taught – corresponds to an episode from Christ's historical life, or even from the whole history of redemption. Thus the Kyrie Eleison was understood as the supplication of the faithful of the old Covenant for the Redeemer, and the blessing at the end of Mass signified Christ's blessing imparted before his ascension.[5]

In these terms the Mass was understood as the *memoria passionis*, as the commemoration of the passion of Christ, not in a sacramental sense, as did the theological schools, but allegorically. People were no longer aware of the historical origin and later evolution. Liturgical instruction appeared to issue from theology only in so far as both interpreted the Mass as a memorial of the passion of Christ. In the more precise understanding of this memorial, liturgical instruction parted company with theological thought and went its own way.

One could not say that the emphasis on the presence in the Mass of Christ's passion and sacrifice led *inevitably* to a stress on the actual performance of the Mass as a rite and therefore to the detriment of the degree of the faithful's participation in it as worship; but in fact this was a consequence.

The question about belief and about intelligent

[5] Cf. J. A. Jungmann, S.J.: *The Eucharistic Prayer* (Challoner, 1956) 12 f.

co-operation in general at the celebration of the Mass decreased in importance. Not infrequently the result was a dangerous work – piety allied to all sorts of superstitious ideas. Adolph Franz has collected numerous examples of this in his book: *Die Messe im deutschen Mittelalter* (1902). Magical notions about the effects of the Mass were not uncommon. Preachers exhorted people to attend Mass more frequently by assuring them that the pains of the holy souls in purgatory were interrupted while someone was praying for them at Mass; and this was by no means the worst aberration.

This inadequate instruction was matched by the sort of participation in public worship. No longer as in the early days did the faithful take active part in the celebration in a manner suited to their status and dignity. That the language of public worship was no longer understood by the people presented an added obstacle in the way of such participation.

The criticism of the Reformers was then launched against the abuses which arose as a result of the lack of active participation by the laity in the liturgy, and as a result of instruction which dwelt in part upon allegory and play-acting, in part upon magical effects. The indictments of the Reformers against the Mass were based not simply upon the theological teaching of the schools, but were provoked predominantly by the practice of the preachers, and by the popular piety which they had engendered. Here we have a most tragic example of how fatal can be the effects of liturgical instruction and education which imag-

ines that it can flourish without being rooted in
fundamental theological thought.

Attempts at reform in the sixteenth century

Seen from the point of view of liturgical education,
the late Middle Ages are characterized by two features. There is a widespread lack of active participation of the faithful in liturgical public worship, and of
liturgical instruction aiming at achieving such participation. This instruction was lacking amongst the
clergy as well as amongst the laity. The terrible
danger of this unhealthy state of affairs was fully
recognized by the humanist reforming Catholicism of
the time; and this movement demanded a remedy.
What were the particular aims of these Catholic
reforming circles? We shall learn exactly what the
wishes and demands of these people were from one of
the most prolific writers and best-known members of
the group, from the priest at Mainz, Georg Witzel (or
as he called himself in Latin, Wicelius), who lived
from 1501 until 1573.[6] Witzel, like his friends, was
concerned with a reform of the pattern of public
worship and of liturgical instruction. Primarily he
demanded an improvement in the liturgical education

[6] Cf. Ludwig Pralle: *Die volksliturgischen Bestrebungen des Georg
Witzel (1501-1573)*, in *Jahrbuch fur das Bistum Mainz*[3] (1948)
224-242; also Rud. Padberg: *Georg Witzel der Ältere, ein
Pastoraltheologe des 16. Jahrhunderts*, in *Theologische Quartal-
schrift* 135 (1955) 385-409.

of the clergy. This, he maintained, must rest upon a scientific foundation, above all upon a knowledge of early Christian worship. Second, there must follow a better liturgical instruction of the laity by means of the sermon. Before every celebration of any sacrament there ought to be a short address on its meaning and on the meaning of the ceremonies. To ensure a better understanding, the texts of the Mass and of the sacraments ought to be translated and read out to the people. Witzel did not rest content with stating these demands: he himself devoted much time and energy to translating these texts. His greatest work of this sort is the *Psaltes Ecclesiasticus* (1550). And yet, he maintained, to enlist the laity in a proper corporate celebration of the Mass it is not enough merely to instruct them and read out translations to them. It is necessary in addition to set about the celebration of Mass and sacraments in such a way that the laity are able to take active part in them. He made a plea for the reinstatement of early Christian public worship. Hence he desired the abolition of purely private Masses. He also demanded that during high Mass there should be no low Masses going on simultaneously. Unfortunately the high Mass was no longer a corporate act of worship by the whole community – so he complained – and the people were no longer permitted to sing their Amen. The congregation ought once again to be given the opportunity to make their appropriate responses, at the very least to be allowed to say the Amen. Likewise he thought it good to revive the Offertory procession, those at least taking part, who intended to receive Communion. Communion ought normally to be distributed during the Mass, along with the priest's Communion in fact. As in the early days, the sick should have Communion taken to them immediately after the celebration of the Mass. Concerning the question of the Cup for the laity, this writer believed that the re-introduction of this practice would be in line with Scripture and the tradition of the Church. In achieving this aim, however, dissension and discord ought not to be aroused within the Church, for the Cup is a symbol of unity, not of division. Witzel was constantly urging the active participation of the laity in the Mass. He gave the laity specific advice on how they could take part in public worship as it then was. He considered that an interior, spiritual participation was not enough.

Arising out of his concern to lead the laity towards active participation in the liturgy, he was bound to come up against the problem of the liturgical language. This problem was much discussed in ecclesiastical humanist circles. The Dutch theologian George Cassander, for example, represented the view that worship should be conducted exclusively in the vernacular, and he based his view on Church history. Witzel did not go so far. It is true that he also thought that it would be an ideal state of affairs if the people understood the language of the liturgy, as they had done in the early Church. There were theologians who claimed dogmatic foundation for Latin as the sole legitimate language, and who wanted to acknowledge only the three so-called *noble* languages in which the inscription on the Cross was written, Hebrew, Greek, and Latin, as liturgical languages. Witzel countered this argument by pointing out that the use of Latin in the liturgy had been a matter of historical evolution. The mother-tongue of the people always had an intrinsic first claim to be the language of worship. In spite of this Witzel was very much in favour of the retention of Latin. Why? He believed that the strange language of the liturgy was a good protection against profanation; but he definitely advocated that the liturgy of prayer and lessons – what we now call the liturgy of the Word – should be conducted in the vernacular.

Not only Witzel but everyone involved at that time in the liturgical movement combined proposals for the reform of public worship with the effort to revive catechetical commentary on the Mass. This was attached to pre-Tridentine theology of the Mass, with most advantageous results. Consequently it abandoned the theatrical allegorization of current preaching. A characteristic of this liturgical instruction was that it clearly expressed the nature of a sacrament. Once more the Mass was seen to be primarily the sacrifice of the whole Church, in which the thought of praise and thanksgiving was often uppermost. The ancient Christian understanding of the Mass as Eucharist, as the festive thanksgiving of the Church in union with Christ, had come to life once again. An integral part of this development was the increased vigour with which men discussed the life of the Church, above all the part played by faith and love as preconditions of a true participation in the celebration.

Thus the period leading up to Trent was a time of fruitful renewal and intensification of liturgical life and thought. Unfortunately we have to assert that almost all of this effort was brought to nothing. What are the reasons for this? Was the time not ripe? It was, in fact, all too ripe. The times were crying out for these very remedies; and the Reformers were applying themselves to the tasks of a people's liturgy with far greater energy. It was so easy for them to pour out their biting contempt for the sometimes miserable state of public worship, and they used the unsolved problems of corporate worship to great effect. For the very reason, indeed, that the Reformers took up liturgical revival and produced radical solutions – we think of the language problem, the Cup for the laity, the priesthood of all believers, etc. – the well-intentioned efforts of pastors who remained loyal to the Church became suspected of aiding and abetting the Reformers, whereas in fact they would have done the exact opposite.

Instruction on the Mass since the Council of Trent

The Council of Trent (1545-63) inaugurated a new epoch. It removed many of the abuses of late medieval worship and of preaching about the Mass, and it laid down for the future the lines which liturgical instruction was to follow. The doctrine of the council concerning the sacrifice of the Mass was conditioned by the new doctrines of the Reformers. The Reformers denied the sacrificial character of the Eucharist: all the more were the Fathers of the Council obliged to stress this aspect. This brought with it the danger of isolating the sacrifice from its old setting within the total picture of the Eucharist. This isolation can be clearly seen in every catechism from Trent until the twentieth century. In these, instruction on the Mass plays only a small part, whereas the dogmatic doctrine, usually in three sections, is in the foreground. This deals first with the true presence of Christ in the sacrament, then with the sacrifice, and third with the Communion – the Eucharist as food. Thus the comprehensive picture which sets the whole field of Eucharistic doctrine within the framework of the sacrament, of the ancient Christian mystery, has been lost sight of for centuries. It is easy to understand how this was not exactly favourable for liturgical education. The thought that the Mass is the Eucharist, the Church's sacrifice of praise and thanksgiving, is obscured by the perfectly correct and legitimate truth that the Mass is Christ's atoning sacrifice.

This shifting of emphasis is seen in another sphere as well. In the expositions of the Mass, the celebrant now appears as the possessor of the special priesthood almost exclusively. From this time on, the fact that the laity, as possessors of the general priesthood, share in public worship is almost never mentioned. Thus the ground was cut from beneath the active participation of the laity in the liturgy. This limitation too is to be seen as a reaction against the Reformers who openly denied that there is a special priesthood, accepting only the general priesthood of all believers. As a result, within the Catholic Church consciousness of the dignity and the function of the general priesthood became stunted, and this led to the surrender of the very basis for all liturgical activity of the faithful. The faithful were now looked upon as the objects, no longer as subjects in the activity of worship. Consequently, even in the majority of modern catechisms, one finds advice on "pious assistance at" Mass, but no guide to active participation.

As in the late Middle Ages so in the seventeenth century popular instruction still followed a course which was based less upon objective facts than upon subjective meanings. Exaggerated, almost magical notions about the fruits of the sacrifice of the Mass were disseminated afresh; once again people delighted in theatrical allegory. Fortunately this description of the seventeenth century requires a correction. A noteworthy, although not the only, exception is the fact that there were groups amongst the French clergy in those days who strove to achieve the active participation of the faithful in the Mass, and this not merely in an interior way, but externally as well. They demanded that the laity should take an active part in the Mass. For example, in 1680 Nicolas Letourneux wrote a book which he called *The Best Way of Hearing Mass*. Of the word "oremus" he writes: "The majority of people have no idea of the meaning of this 'oremus', which we use so frequently in the celebration of the sacrifice. It is supposed to signify that you must join in the prayer of the priest, which you are offering through him, and ought not to be engaging in private prayers. This is not the time for such prayers. While the priest is praying all other prayers must be silent."[7] Amongst the French clerical circles of that period, who sought to bring about a revival of public worship, there was the desire to use the vernacular in part of the Mass in order to enable the laity to take an active part in it. Thus the problem of the language of the liturgy is not a typically German problem, but a problem for the whole Church, as is proved today by the missions. This problem emerges in every place where people are in earnest about giving public worship an intelligible, communal shape.

The French pastors of the seventeenth century were by no means only interested in the laity taking an active part in the liturgy. They were very much concerned also that the dominant thought and supreme aim of the liturgy must be the glory of God. This was what gave rise to their demand that Sunday as the day of the Lord ought not to be ousted by saints' days. In line with this demand was the proposal that the Word of God, the Scriptures of the Old and the New Testament, ought to provide much

[7] Cf. W. Trapp: *Vorgeschichte und Ursprung der liturgischen Bewegung vorwiegend in Hinsicht auf das deutsche Sprachgebiet* (Würzburg 1939) 9 f.

more of the content of the liturgy, particularly of the Divine Office. All that is purely legendary must be removed from the liturgy. This applied principally to part of the lessons at Matins. This is a hope which indeed plays its part also in the modern plan for a reform of the Breviary.

Liturgical education under the influence of the Enlightenment

Apart from the present time no period in the Church's history has shown such a lively interest in questions relating to liturgical life as did the age of the Enlightenment. At that time books and articles on problems concerning the reform of public worship and liturgical instruction appeared in profusion. Interest in schemes of reform was widespread and the problems were discussed with unusual frankness. As in the theological, philosophical, and educational spheres so in that of liturgical studies there were two tendencies, one radical, the other moderate. The aims of all were essentially the same; only, on the one hand they were advanced radically, on the other in a more moderate way. These aims were in part the same as we have already met in the humanists of the sixteenth century: active and intelligent participation of the faithful in public worship, especially in the Mass; the recovery of the Mass as a celebration of the whole congregation; a consideration of the use – at least in part – of the vernacular; a stress on the liturgy rather than on popular devotions; the demand for a much more important place for holy Scripture in worship; a war against all dead formalism, against a purely mechanical administration of the sacraments, and the insistence on essentials or, in the language of the Enlightenment, on rationality. All these things had been live issues in the earlier period.

Like the enthusiastic humanist reformers of the sixteenth century, those of the Enlightenment put forward two basic demands in order to achieve a proper liturgical attitude in clergy and laity. There must be a better liturgical *enlightenment* of the laity, and the active participation of the congregation in public worship.

Complaints were still heard that the faithful did not understand the liturgical celebrations and actions, or that they misunderstood them in a superstitious fashion. Liturgical essays, combating this, were constantly urging the clergy to pay heed to the decrees of the Council of Trent, to introduce the laity to the Mass, to explain to them the meaning of the feasts of the Christian Year and of the ceremonies. Priests were exhorted to preach frequently at Mass. One theologian, Franz Oberthur, professor of dogmatics in Würzburg, even affirmed the principle that a priest should never say Mass without preaching a short discourse.[8] Following the spirit of the Enlightenment, the importance of instruction was overstressed. Sometimes instruction was regarded as more important than the liturgical actions themselves. A

[8] Cf. W. Trapp: *op. cit.* 38.

definite emphasis was laid upon understanding, that
is to say upon rational knowledge. This motive is the
clue to understanding the passion with which the
right of the vernacular within the Church was
championed. The desire that the vernacular be recognized in worship was universal. Benedict Maria
Werkmeister (1745-1823), originally a Benedictine in
the monastery of Weresheim and later the court-
preacher in Stuttgart, spokesman of the radical party,
put forward an extreme solution. He thought that
the whole liturgy should be celebrated in German.
This alone, he wrote, was "the simplest, the happiest,
the most direct and only means of removing all
difficulties".[9] He was not the only one who demanded
and practised such a solution. The majority by far,
however, were in favour of a middle course, asking
that those parts of the Mass, of the sacraments and of
the sacramentals, that came specially before the
people should be conducted in German. This view
was expressed by no less men than the leading
theologians of the time, John Michael Sailer, John
Baptist Hirscher, and John Adam Möhler. Sailer,
always moved by his irenic disposition towards mediation and compromise, opposed equally those who
believed that all salvation lay in translating the
liturgical texts into German, and those who exalted
the complete retention of Latin into a dogma. He
admittedly had a vision of a liturgy in German
sometime in the future. In one passage in his book,

[9] *Beiträge zur Verbesserung der Katholischen Liturgie in Deutsch-
land* (1789) 346 f.

Neue Beiträge zur Bildung des Geistlichen,[10] he expresses this view, writing of the "basic, mother-tongue of worship", by which he means not the uttering of words, but the whole physical expression at worship which hears and enlivens the words. He says: "Some day when German priests say Mass in the German tongue, then the German word, brought to life by the basic, mother-tongue of worship, will take hold of the mind and understanding, the reason and the heart of the people, and priest and people will be one loving heart, one praying soul."

The problem of the liturgical language has already brought us to the subject of the form of public worship. The driving force here was the determination to put an end to the liturgy as a preserve of the clergy and make it a celebration of the whole congregation. The status of the ordained priest remained unassailed throughout. Various and repeatedly expressed proposals helped towards this goal. There appeared hymns for Mass and Vespers in the German language. Specially well-known are the Vespers of Ignatius Henry of Wessenberg, Vicar-general of Constance, which are still sung in many parishes in Switzerland and Baden.

Naturally it was urged that the faithful should receive Communion along with the priest, that is neither before nor after Mass, but during Mass and not before the priest's Communion. Private Masses celebrated while the Mass for the faithful was in

[10] (1809-11) I 252 f.

progress was felt to be a distraction. This practice was opposed, not merely in a literary way, but occasionally through prohibition by the authorities. Thus, for example, on February 25, 1783, a police regulation governing public worship was issued in Vienna, prohibiting the saying of several Masses in one church at the one time. The same prohibition was promulgated for the churches in Munich on October 27, 1827.

The arrangement of the place of worship too was discussed from the point of view of the communal character of the liturgy. Vitus Anthony Winter (1750-1814), professor of theology and a parish priest in Landshut, one of the active reformers, proposed amongst other things that to achieve a better participation by the faithful, the altar, as in early Christian times, should be erected so that the priest was facing the congregation.[11] So that architectural expression be given to the unity of the celebration of the Mass, and to ensure that unity, on January 7, 1785, the Austrian government ordained that all new churches must be equipped with only one altar.[12] These and similar regulations must, of course, be seen against the caesaropapism of the established Church of the period. On the other hand these regulations prove how widespread was the desire for reform.

If we survey this whole period of the Enlighten-

---

[11] *Erstes deutsches kritisches Messbuch* (1810) 320.
[12] W. Trapp: *op. cit.* 26.

ment with its most varied activity in the field of
liturgy, we might be inclined to think that the
liturgical movement of that time was very much in
line with that of our own day. But that is not so. It
is true that there is a similarity in many of the
particular desires and practical proposals; but it is
only a superficial resemblance. At a deeper level there
is a difference. The motives for the liturgical efforts
of the Enlightenment were basically different from
our motives today. When, for example, the Enlightenment eagerly appealed to the early Church, the
motive was not a desire to find in her the Christian
depth and the wealth of supernatural substance of
the liturgy. It was rather that they extolled the early
Christian period as the ideal because they found less
to offend the spirit of the Enlightenment there than
in the Middle Ages. They thought that there they
found again their own notions about *rational worship*.
Anything which did not agree with their own ideas,
they disregarded. Because the Enlightenment in
general lacked any sense of history or tradition, it
lacked also an understanding of the historical evolution of the Church's liturgy. An example will illustrate the contrast. The stress on community did not
arise from a perception of the Church as the *corpus
Christi mysticum*, but from the simple consideration
that the people would be edified better by taking
part in a communal act of worship than by merely
looking on. The same thing applied to the demand for
the suppression of private Masses and side altars.
This arose, not from a supernatural concept of com-

munity, but because it was thought that this would be the way to teach and edify the people more effectively. Men may have been striving to give the liturgy pride of place above popular devotions and religious custom; but this was not done from a deep insight into the nature of the liturgy. The rationalist and moralistic spirit of the Enlightenment could scarcely understand the practice of the Church. The nature of the liturgy was seen primarily in terms of expedience. The purpose of the liturgy, on these terms, was to make people better. Thus we are dealing with an anthropocentric concept of the liturgy. For the Enlightenment, the highest aim of religion was the morality of man. This goal was thought to be soonest attained by means of a *natural* and rational *enlightenment* and a *logically* designed worship.

And so the comparison of the reforming attempts of the Enlightenment with those of our own time shows only an external agreement. Fundamentally they differ on almost every point; on many they are even in direct contradiction. We must qualify this statement, however. In respect of motives, the liturgical efforts of the Enlightenment are not to be reduced to a single common denominator. The above statements apply only with qualification, in some cases not at all, to the moderate party. The direct contrasts which have been expounded are taken from the picture presented by radical Enlightenment in the Church.

The liturgical revival today

The apparent similarity between the liturgical endeavours of the Enlightenment and those of today poses the question whether or not the efforts at reform today have their origin in those of a hundred and fifty years ago. There seems, however, to be no historical connection. The liturgical endeavours of a hundred and fifty years ago remained limited within their own age. They have left no trace of any influence on the second half of the nineteenth century. On the contrary, the period of the restoration of the Church set itself consciously against the earlier attempts at liturgical reform.

Liturgical education during the second half of the nineteenth century consisted predominantly of instruction about the liturgy. In contrast to the Enlightenment its strength lay in that it gave a deeper and more essential meaning to the liturgy. Its weakness lay in the too theoretical manner in which it took up the tasks of practical arrangements, in contrast to the great zeal of the Enlightenment on these matters. The demand that the laity be led to share in the Mass no longer meant that the laity be urged to take active part in the celebration. The aim becomes merely to guide them towards devout following of the Mass. Typical of this aim is the catechism of Joseph Deharbe, S.J., which dominated catechetical instruction in Germany from the middle of the nineteenth century. He expounds the second commandment of the Church by the following question: "What are we commanded by the second commandment? To assist at holy Mass on all Sundays and holidays of obligation with due attention, reverence, and devotion." The next question underlines the externally passive role of the faithful at Mass: "Why is the hearing of Mass the chief thing commanded on Sundays and holidays?"[13]

The various translations of the Missal were designed to serve the same purpose of *devout* attendance. That of the Beuron Benedictine, Anselm Schott, which first appeared in 1884, ran into far more editions than any other.

As we have already said, the period after 1850 was not a continuation of an earlier liturgical movement. It was not a continuation even in the sense that it rejected the immoderate and unlimited reforms of the Enlightenment, but took up those which were justified. This period stood much more in conscious contradiction to the previous one. This meant that the numerous open questions and tasks remained unresolved. That they also remained undiscussed was proved by the next period in liturgical education which began after the First World War and in the midst of which we now live. This is the period of the so-called Liturgical Movement. This phrase is to be found, indeed, in the preface to the Vesperale by A. Schott, O.S.B., which appeared in 1893. But it was far too optimistic to speak then of a *movement*.

---

[13] *Grosser katholischer Katechismus mit einem Abriss der Religionsgeschichte für die reifere Jugend und für Erwachsene* (Regensburg 1860).

The Liturgical Movement at the end of the nineteenth and the beginning of the twentieth century could count only single and solitary advance guards. It appeared in Germany as a genuine movement after the First World War. In Germany its enthusiasts and first advocates were chiefly the Benedictine monasteries of Beuron and Maria-Laach, the Catholic Youth Movement groups, especially those who met under the leadership of R. Guardini at Burg Rothenfels, circles of the Catholic Academic Union, and individuals such as Pius Parsch, master of the Augustine Choir at Klosterneuberg, near Vienna.

Many of the aims of the contemporary liturgical revival resemble those of earlier attempts at reform. There is no need to describe them in detail here because they will be dealt with fully in the systematic exposition. In contrast to the attempts at liturgical reform in earlier centuries, the Liturgical Movement of the twentieth century is marked, even externally, by two factors: it enjoys an unusually wide appeal and a hitherto unknown support from the leaders of the Church.

Above all, since the 'thirties the Liturgical Movement has not only spread widely in clerical circles, but also amongst the laity, especially amongst teachers. This scope is something new in the history of the liturgy. It is no longer little groups of interested priests and esoteric lay circles that have a special feeling for the liturgy. Much more it is now a case of a considerable number of priests and active laity possessed by the intention to make again of the liturgy of the Church what it has always been in essence: the public worship of the whole people of God, priest together with people, the chief source of the Christian life. This broad stream of liturgical revival only makes sense when understood against the background of the total spiritual situation today. That cannot be described in detail here. In the course of this book, however, several opportunities will occur of drawing attention to these inter-relations. In the words of R. Guardini, from inner necessity the time has become ripe for the liturgy.[14] This is the reason also for the amazing fact that the liturgical revival is not restricted to Germany but inspires the whole Church, if perhaps in varying degrees in different places. Besides this it is encountered in all large Christian communities. It is not limited to one continent, much less to one country. Obviously there are differences, even great differences; obviously there is resistance everywhere to the movement. How could it be otherwise? But everywhere we can see a longing for a deepened and more basic understanding of, a living and active participation in, public worship.

The second characteristic feature of the modern Liturgical Movement is that it does not exist in opposition to Church leadership, but is blessed by it, encouraged by it, had been to some extent inaugurated by it. It was Pius X in his *Motu Proprio* of 1903 who made the demand for the "actuosa participatio", for the active participation of the faithful in the celebration of the mysteries. This was in the *Motu*

[14] *Liturgischer Bildung* (1923) 13.

Proprio of November 22, 1903, concerning Church music. The noteworthy passage runs: "And since indeed Our first and most ardent wish is that a true Christian spirit flourish and be kept always by all the faithful, the first thing to which We must attend is the holiness and dignity of the churches in which our people assemble, in order to acquire that spirit from its first and most indispensable source, by taking an active part in the sacred mysteries and in the solemn public prayers of the Church."[15] The statement of Pius XI in his apostolic constitution *Divini cultus* of 1928, that it is no longer good enough for the faithful to attend worship as silent spectators, is well-known. But no Papal document has provided such encouragement and exhortation for the Liturgical Movement as the encyclical of Pius XII on the liturgy: *Mediator Dei* (November 20, 1947).

That the Popes have declared themselves for the Liturgical Movement signifies an authoritative protection for the movement, and the possibility of its evolution through peaceful and undisturbed growth. This is precisely what it needs if it is to produce permanent gain for the Church.[16]

---

[15] *Motu Proprio of Pope Pius the Tenth on Sacred Music*, London, Catholic Truth Society, 1905.

[16] Even more authoritative support has been given to the Liturgical Movement by the *Constitution on the Sacred Liturgy*, promulgated in 1963 after this book was written. Appropriate references to this *Constitution* are given in footnotes.

II

THE CONCEPT OF LITURGICAL EDUCATION

IN 1923 Romano Guardini published his book *Liturgische Bildung*. In this he tried to deepen and to particularize the ideas he had developed in 1918 in his book *Vom Geist der Liturgie*.[1] Whereas by 1953 this book had reached its eighteenth edition and by 1957 had been put in a cheap paper-back series, the earlier work was printed in a single edition. The discrepancy is striking and noteworthy, for the tasks facing liturgical education, as Guardini saw them in 1923, had been solved only in the smallest degree, in spite of three decades of liturgical revival. Their urgency remains unabated today.

In the book, *Liturgische Bildung*, Romano Guardini sees the situation and its tasks like this. The first phase of the Liturgical Movement is finished. That was the time when the greatness and beauty of the liturgy had been discovered. Now, however – that is in 1923 – the task is to revive the liturgical life of the parishes. It is here that the greatest difficulties are to be expected, and here too are to be found the real tasks of liturgical education; for faithful and pastors alike no longer possess the mental attitude, the sense of life, which corresponds to the liturgy of the Church. The men of the Middle Ages still had it. They were

[1] *The Spirit of the Liturgy*, London 1930.

still capable of seeing and creating symbols; for these
men were still living within the lively unity of spirit
and body, of individual and community, of man and
the world. By contrast, modern times have lost this
unity, this tension. The result has been the separation
into the two extremes of a dualistic or a monistic
interpretation of existence. The piety of the faithful
has been profoundly influenced by this development,
so that they have lost a living relationship to what is
genuinely liturgical. Modern times, however, are now
ended. A change has dawned in Western thought –
and not only there. Man once again desires the unity
of spirit and body; he is tired of his isolated, individualistic existence, and presses violently on towards
community and to an objective grasp of things. This
new vitality contains hidden within itself the natural
preconditions for a liturgical attitude. Hence, by an
inner necessity, the time is becoming ripe for the
liturgy. It is now, however, of great moment, whether
or not these newly-awakened powers will find their
way to the liturgy of the Church. Here at the heart
of the Church's life the decisions of our time will be
made. Thus the liturgical problem is one of the most
pressing for our ecclesiastical and cultural future.
The solution certainly demands an education of man
in terms of the liturgy – liturgical education indeed.
This means more than just a knowledge of liturgical
matters: it comprises a formation of the whole man,
of his mind and his body.

At this point let us cease following Guardini's line
of thought. Much that has been quoted from Guar-

dini's thought has been confirmed, and much realized, since he wrote. However great the achievement to date has been, the fundamental concerns of liturgical education as Guardini represented them in 1923 have not thereby been rendered obsolete. Quite the opposite: today they have taken on a much greater urgency, because lively activity in the liturgical sphere is developing in countless parishes.

The following exposition of some of the fundamental questions of liturgical education cannot, and does not, claim to offer valid solutions to the problems. It is merely an attempt to clarify some of the basic questions and tasks facing liturgical education. From the discussion of these questions and tasks must arise the clarification of the concept of liturgical education. First of all, therefore, we must make clear what exactly we mean by the term "liturgical education".

The concept of education

Both common and scientific speech use the word "education" to denote sometimes the process of education and sometimes the state of being educated which results from this process. We say, for example, that the teacher educates the pupil by instruction and schooling. This is education as an activity directed towards an end. As we have said, however, people call the end itself education. Thus we speak of seeking a *higher education* or of having attained an *academic education*. This double sense of the word "education" – meaning education as a process and as a condition – is now applied to the most varied meanings of the word. According to the still dominant view education is chiefly a matter of knowing. The more a person knows the more educated he appears to be. Because one's knowledge is certified through examinations, one's degree of education rises with every examination passed. The notion is still widespread that only so-called *academic education* is entitled to the name of true education. On this view the academic man is the educated man; the academically educated, as people like to say, is the fully educated. Nonetheless, a modicum of education is recognized in the non-academic type. This, however, is a distortion of the concept of education. How uneducated can such an educated man be in reality, and, in contrast, how truly educated a peasant, a labourer, a craftsman! But even setting aside this gross misunder·standing, the whole of modern times has been characterized by the idea that education consists primarily in the acquisition of knowledge mediated through an educational heritage. Hence education comes through instruction. It is in line with this intellectualist concept of education to speak, by contrast, of *physical education*, by which for the most part we mean bodily exercise, that is training in sports. As a rule such physical education has nothing whatever to do with the education of the mind. It is concerned purely and simply with a body thoroughly trained for and capable of sport.

Both concepts of education contradict the nature of man. Man is neither pure spirit nor sheer body. He is spirit and body; and these two are not there merely in external juxtaposition. Man's nature consists in his being a living unity of spirit and body. He is not pure spirit, but a spirit moulded by flesh, by sense: and his body is formed by the spirit. And so education in the true sense means a formation of the whole man. Education means the moulding of a spirit which works itself out in a unified form through the body and all its senses. Concepts such as intellectual education, character training, and physical education, are thus contradictions of the true meaning of education. Education covers all of these, not in unrelated isolation from each other, but as a single process and a unified thing. This formation is like a *picture*. In German the word for education means literally "making a picture". The idea behind education is, therefore, that man is a picture or that he is supposed to become one. This signifies that man is a visible unity, a form moulded from within and capable of being seen.

Contemporary philosophy and pedagogics look with suspicion upon such a concept of education. There may be various reasons for this suspicion. Very common is the uneasiness born of the fear that such a view of man's nature might deny the individual the right to the concrete reality within which he exists. Rejection of this concept of education results, then, from the fear that an abstract ideal is being proposed that is not in accord with the being and the situation

of actual men. There is much to justify such fears.
The history of education, especially of modern education can show many bitter experiences with educational ideals and principles. But when we think of
man as a *picture* and of human life as *being a picture*
we are not thinking of this as an abstract ideal which
is imposed upon man with no regard for the fact that
every man is determined by his uniqueness and his
concrete situation. We think of "picture" so that all
that goes to make up the individual is included, not
only his essence but also his concrete actualization in
his predicament.

Finally, however, part of the picture of man in this
concrete sense is that he is created and called to life by
God. Man is not autonomous. The concept of autonomous man is a nebulous abstraction precisely
because it contradicts the reality of man. Man does
not subsist in himself; he is not a being who rests and
is complete in himself. The understanding of man as
a picture points to the relationship of man to God as
his creator and source. Man as creature is a picture
or image of his creator. We say that he is a likeness or
a copy of God (cf. Genesis 1:26 f). It is most important
to make clear that man is already this by nature, not
only through the Christian faith. By faith, that is by
grace, this likeness which was obscured and distorted
by sin is restored and intensified in its original purity
through men sharing in Christ the "image of the
invisible God" (Col. 1:15). Man becomes this sort of
image of God by means of the liturgy of the Church;
for in the liturgy the redemptive action of Christ,

the Son and image of the Father, is made present. By receiving this action in faith man regains his original *health*, his original state of likeness.

Thus it is God, through Christ in the power of his Spirit, who restores man to be his living image or *picture* upon this earth. Without this prevenient action of God there is no true education of any real depth. The man who is being educated and those who are helping him in that work are all engaged in this activity of becoming an image. When we speak of liturgical education it is this human aspect of education that we have in mind.

Education as living knowledge

We shall elucidate this understanding of liturgical education with an idea we owe to Otto Willmann. In his chief work *Didaktik als Bildungslehre* he puts forward a concept of education having three components: living knowledge, spiritualized skill, and purified will.[2]

According to this, the first requirement of liturgical education is living knowledge.

The liturgy is a great and holy thing, comprising a wealth of practices, actions, things and texts. One cannot adopt the proper attitude to this reality unless one has a practical knowledge of it. By *practical* we do not necessarily mean that knowledge must be

[2] 3 (1903) II 48 f.

scientific. This knowledge can be gained entirely by way of popular, unreflective thought, but – and this is the point – it must be knowledge that corresponds to its object. What is this object which must be known? It is the reality of the Church's worshipping life. In other words, the knowledge of the liturgical reality must be controlled by its object. This knowledge must not take its origin in the caprice of subjective opinion and invention. For example: the proper celebration of the Christian Year demands a working knowledge of the whole year of our Lord, as well as of the separate festivals. Such knowledge can only be acquired, however, if one takes the liturgical texts seriously. But those very seasons and feasts of the Church are often interpreted according to subjective ideas, and with no regard to the texts which reflect the mind of the Church. The results are what we might expect.

And so the first demand of liturgical education is this. People must be given a working knowledge of the Church's public worship. A necessary precondition of this is that the educator or instructor first of all makes an honest effort to gain a knowledge of this sort for himself.

One element of true education, according to Otto Willmann, is *living* knowledge. What is meant by that? Following the metaphor, a living knowledge is to be contrasted with dead knowledge. Dead knowledge is knowledge learnt parrot-wise, stored up in the memory, for examinations it may be, only to be forgotten thereafter. By contrast living knowledge arises out of a true encounter, and increases in insight through ever renewed encounters. Liturgical education ought to be of this kind. In its inmost mystery the public worship of the Church is an event of the most intense vitality. This can be taken hold of only if the human spirit responds to the mystery with the appropriate receptivity and life. In this context, *living* means that the human spirit is engaged in true *perception*, in knowledge in the sense of real experience and encounter. The believer takes part over and over again, it may be every day, in the public worship of the Church. In this way his knowledge of worship gains depth and fulness and keeps alive. At least this is the meaning of participation. Obviously there is such a thing as dead knowledge in this sphere. There is a study of the liturgy that is purely historical, having a merely theoretical or aesthetic interest; but the knowledge possessed by the man who wants to share in the Church's worship in the right way must not be of this cold, basically disinterested, kind. It must be living knowledge.

The characterization of this knowledge as *living* could be misunderstood. One might take this living quality to lie in the irrational, especially in the emotional, origin of this knowledge. Hence it might be said to follow that this knowledge was suffering from a serious lack of objectivity. This would be in contradiction to the initial principle that liturgical knowledge must be, first and foremost, objective and corresponding to reality. To be living indicates anything but a diminished grade of reality. It is rather the very opposite which is meant. Knowledge that leads straight to an encounter with reality is the knowledge that is truly alive. Mere learning by rote never leads further than introductory knowledge in any sphere. This is particularly true of the sphere of worship. The mystery of Christian worship is no corpse to be understood as a result of anatomical dissection. It is a reality of the highest spiritual vitality. Hence any kind of thought-process which does not involve true encounter is of no use as a means of comprehending it.

Education as a spiritualized skill

According to Otto Willmann, this is the second requirement of genuine education.

True education does not stop at knowledge. Knowledge is certainly no mere precondition; it is part of the substance of education itself. The truly educated man is a knowledgeable man; but he is not just that. The truly educated man is a man formed in accordance with his total reality. As we have said already, perfect education consists in the formation of all a man's capacities, mental, spiritual, and physical.

Applied to liturgical education this means that the liturgy is no system of teaching and no mere conceptual scheme. It is an entity of a spiritual and a material kind. Its core is spiritual and hence invisible, its husk material and hence visible; but the invisible core only exists along with the visible husk. As a result, liturgical activity is not something purely spiritual. The liturgy has to do not with mere thinking but with doing; and this doing is always physical action. This activity makes demands upon the whole man, upon both his spiritual and sensory faculties. All the body's senses are brought into play. The man looks, listens, speaks, and sings; he walks, stands, kneels, and sits down. Liturgical activity is full of sacred movements: bowing, folding the hands, outstretching the arms, blessings, crossing oneself. In the sacraments a man is purified by water, anointed with oil, and nourished with bread and wine.

All that is performed in such visible, physical actions has a prescribed form. Consequently one must be able to do these things and so must practise them. Nonetheless this must be a capability which is infused with the spirit. Routine, either of priest or altar-servers, is not enough. The form must be inspired by an understanding of what is being done. The meaning of what is going on at the particular moment must be recognized. This inspiration does not imply a neglect of the outward form. We dare not say: the form is unimportant, all that matters is the spiritual interior, the essence. No, both are important, the interior and the external. Man is not all spirit, just as he is not all body. Both go to make up the nature of man. Hence we must pay close heed to outward form. It is not beside the point which attitude a man adopts at prayer, how the liturgy is performed in the house of God, how a man stands at the altar, imparts the blessing, distributes the Eucharistic bread. A bad external attitude does not necessarily imply a well-disposed spirit. As a rule the interior and the external form a unity. What is interior seeks expression, and physical activities affect the spirit.

And so liturgical education demands a regulated and orderly bodily attitude, a visible, audible activity moulded by the spirit. It demands a spiritualized skill.

Education as purified will

Education would be mere illusion if not pursued with moral determination. However important knowledge, however necessary accomplishment, we would never designate a man "educated" whose will had not been purified. There is no true education which does not include a mentality controlled by morality. Moral earnestness belongs to the nature of the educated man. Education is thus not merely organic development but a matter of moral effort. Without the decision for good and against evil there is no education. This decision, moreover, cannot be made once and for all: it must be made over and over again. Man is not a plant, not an animal. His perfection is not accomplished purely biologically but personally: it is won only through his own self-determination.

The liturgy is a sacred reality commanding reverence. Hidden within itself it contains nothing less than the presence of the holy God himself. Thus a man may take part in worship only in a frame of mind which is attuned to this holiness. This frame of mind includes: reverence before the mystery of the divine presence; purity before the holiness of God; seriousness – for it is a question of salvation; contrition – for man appears before God always as a sinner; but also joyful trust in the forgiving God, and finally, bringing all the rest to life, the mind of Christian love, for the deepest mystery of God is love. This is what comes to mankind through the mysteries of the Church. But this love demands the same disposition in men, not merely love of God, but – for the two are inseparable – love of one's fellow men as well, especially love of those within the household of faith, those who share in the celebration of the mysteries.

There can be no liturgical education unless men are educated in this attitude of mind. In the liturgy our prime concern is not aesthetically faultless forms. In the liturgy one should be meeting the holy and gracious God himself; and of necessity this presupposes a spiritual preparation, a preparation of attitude.

Looking soberly at the public worship in our parishes we see what tasks lie ahead. A congregation having mightily impressive Communion statistics is not always a congregation carrying out the public worship of the Church in the right frame of mind. On the other hand, quite obviously, a congregation with bad attendance at Communion is not therefore a congregation showing a great reverence for the holiness of God. A priest who serves his congregation with joy and meekness, as an example and not as lording it over them, as St. Peter describes it (1 Pet. 5:1-4), possesses a necessary precondition of his being a good minister of the liturgy.

One last example: a training for altar servers which does not educate them in reverence in the house of God, fails in its essential object.

Let us review our thoughts and so round off our picture of the man who takes part in the public worship of the Church in the right way. We see the picture of a man who is educated for worship according to the fulness of his being, in a living unity of soul and body, and who allows himself to be formed by that worship. This must be a formation of the whole man as we have described it in terms of three requirements. Liturgical education consists in living knowledge, spiritualized skill, and a purified will.[3]

[3] Cf. *Const.*, Arts. 2, 14f, 18, 19.

III

THE ESSENCE OF THE LITURGY

IN the book entitled *Totale Bildung* (Total Education) produced in 1935 by J. Pieper and H. Raskop, the thesis is stated in connection with St. Thomas Aquinas, that we can attribute genuine education only to the man who possesses a comprehensive view of the whole of reality. By this comprehensive view the authors do not mean that one should know every separate detail of all reality, for such a thing would be impossible. That man has a comprehensive view, however, who grasps reality as a whole and as a unity. The man who synthesizes the multiplicity and variety of things into a unified whole alone possesses true education. The man who does not have this view over all things cannot be said to be educated in the true sense, even if he commands great specialist knowledge.

The human mind is adapted to perceive totality. In the *Summa Theologica* St. Thomas Aquinas says: "man desires to know something whole and perfect".[1] St. Augustine's experience was the same, as he records in his *Confessions* (4, 11): ". . . all collectively would please more than they do severally, could all be perceived collectively".

[1] *Summa Theologica* I-II, q.xxxii, a. Translation by English Dominicans, published by R. & T. Washbourne, London 1914 Part II (First Part), First Number, p.375.

49

This demand for a comprehensive view applies not only to reality as a whole, but to its separate spheres also. From time to time the mind of man desires to and ought to become aware of the separate spheres of reality each in its totality. Applying this thesis to the liturgy we can assert that it is of the nature of liturgical education to have a comprehensive view of the reality which is the liturgy. Such a comprehensive view does not consist in knowing every detail of the liturgy, but rather in recognizing the unity behind the variety of liturgical actions, and so seeing the whole. The core of all, however, which is common to everything, is the essence of the liturgy. Knowledge of the essence thus imparts knowledge of the totality of the liturgy. What, then, is the essence of the liturgy?

Insight into the essence

The papal encyclical on the liturgy, *Mediator Dei*, defines the liturgy as "the public worship which our Redeemer, the Head of the Church, offers to the heavenly Father and which the community of Christ's faithful pays to its Founder, and through Him to the Eternal Father; briefly it is the whole public worship of the Mystical Body of Jesus Christ, Head and members".[2]

[2] *Christian Worship*, London, Catholic Truth Society, 1947, section 20. Cf. *Const.*, arts. 2, 6, 7.

Fellowship between God and man was destroyed by the Fall. Man of himself was incapable of making atonement to God, of giving him due honour, or of delivering himself from everlasting death. These things could be done by God alone. In Christ the love of God appeared as the saving and life-giving power which delivers man from sin and everlasting death, restores him to eternal life, making him capable of honouring God and serving him with devotion. The Incarnation means that God himself comes, through his Son, to perform the work of the salvation of the whole of mankind. The entire life of Christ is the work of the Son by which he glorifies the Father and redeems mankind.[3] This work is consummated in the death and exaltation of Christ. What remains to be done is the application of this work to mankind. Ever since the first feast of Pentecost the glorified Lord has been applying his redemptive work to men by the Holy Spirit through the visible forms of sacramental actions. This redemptive work of Christ in the public worship of the Church is called liturgy. This meaning is derived from the Greek phrase *leiton ergon* which originally meant "work for the people". By this was denoted something performed by someone for the good of all. The original meaning fits Christian worship exactly in so far as it is Christ who, by this worship, effects the redemption of mankind. Consequently the word "liturgy" reminds us that the redemptive work of Christ is the central mystery of

[3] Cf. *Const.*, art. 5.

the liturgy. As we have seen, the supreme place of Christ's activity in the liturgy is stressed in the encyclical *Mediator Dei*.

But the greatness of Christ's redemptive work does not ultimately consist in the fact that by it man is made capable once again of honouring God in the right and perfect way. It is in faithful union with Christ that the Church is able to offer this glory to God. This above all is what happens in public worship. We must therefore understand this activity of the Church as part of the essence of the liturgy.[4]

The definition given by the encyclical stresses yet another factor. The liturgy is not simply the worship of Christ and the Church, but the *public* worship of Christ and the Church. The idea of public worship brings out the contrast with private worship. Private worship comprises not only the form of individual personal piety, but also so-called *devotions*. By contrast the *liturgy* comprises the sacraments, the sacramentals, and the Divine Office.

The importance of insight into the essence

What is the importance of an insight into the essence of the liturgy for the tasks facing liturgical education?

At the beginning, in connection with the booklet *Totale Bildung* by Pieper-Raskop, we spoke of the fundamental importance in education of a comprehensive view of things. Such an insight as we have gained into the essence of the liturgy gives us this

[4] Cf. *Const.*, art. 7.

comprehensive view. The believer who possesses this insight comprehends the whole of the liturgy in a unified and integrating picture. He does not merely see the separate parts; he does not merely know about this or that ceremony; he knows what the whole thing is about. Thus, for example, he does not see each separate sacrament in isolation, but sees the seven sacraments as a single great, meaningful entity. Beholding the action of Christ in all of the sacraments, with the eye of the spirit he sees the single stream of divine activity. In this way is regained the ancient Christian awareness of the Lord present and active in his mysteries.

In spite of a unified view, the peculiarities of the separate sacraments are not overlooked. The action of Christ in Baptism, let us say, is different from his action in the Eucharist; nor is his action the same in Confirmation as in Holy Order. But the various peculiarities all rise upon one common foundation. The world of sacramentals, too, receives its integration within the whole of worship through an insight into the essence of the liturgy. The sacramentals are not to be set on the same plane as the sacraments, nonetheless the presence of the Lord at work within and upon the Church is effective in them also. Consecrations and blessings are in particular danger of being regarded in isolation as things in their own right; and because people love to receive them it is important not only to explain the various ceremonies, but also to illumine their connection with the whole world of the sacramentals.

By gaining insight into the essence of the liturgy the worship of the Church is seen to be a unified whole. In this way one of the basic requirements of liturgical education is fulfilled; for a liturgical education which attends only to details and does not provide a survey of the whole field of the liturgy is not fulfilling its true function.

Admittedly the Christological understanding of the essence of the liturgy is not exhausted with the gaining of a unified view. It is seen over and above this in the supremely important activity of *discerning what is specifically Christian*.

Every religion has its cult. In many respects these cults differ, but the essential thing, giving tangible expression to a corporate honouring of God, unites them all. From this we might infer that the liturgy of the Church is to be understood merely as one among many cults. On this view we would place Christian worship within the series of all the other cults known to mankind – perhaps setting it at the peak of the development. Thus evaluated, Christian worship would not be essentially distinguished from the rest of the cults. In its core, however, the Christian liturgy is something essentially different from all other cults known to the history of religion. The Christian liturgy is on the same plane as other cults just as little as the Christian religion is only one amongst the other religions of mankind. Just as the Christian faith has not emerged *from below* out of the religious instincts and aspirations of men, but presupposes the revelation of the one, living God, so in its essence, that is in its true core, the liturgy is not a product of the human spirit. In accordance with its substance it is *from above*. This substance consists, in fact, of God's redemptive activity, revealed in Jesus Christ. Consequently the liturgy does not belong to the series of cults. From the point of view merely of the history of religion it certainly presents a wealth of material which suggest relationships with other cults. This follows from the fact that the liturgy is not only the action of God in Christ, but is also human activity and effort. Again, the Church has adopted many forms of worship from other religions and filled them with a fresh content.

Understanding the essence of the liturgy is obstructed, therefore, when the believer sees it as a purely natural phenomenon. On the other hand he is helped to understand it by recognizing the unique, peculiar greatness of the Church's liturgy. He sees it as a supernatural thing, instituted and sustained by God.

If, following a concept of liturgy inherited from the Enlightenment, we see the Church's worship as a purely natural cult, we are committed thereby to the idea that this worship is – at least for the most part – a human activity. Now the action of the priest, now that of the people can assume the greater importance; but all the time, or on the whole, we are concerned with what men are doing. And so we use the phrase "divine service" in this sense too. By it we mean the service man renders to God, the practice of the virtue of religion. Actual experience confirms this sense of the phrase. Divine service is undoubtedly from start to finish a human activity: speaking, singing, sacrificing, receiving.

On the other hand, if liturgy is understood in terms of its real mystery as the presence of the operation of Christ, values are completely reversed. The liturgy then appears as primarily the action of God, and only secondarily as the action of man. We are not concerned with the visible actions but with the true substance. This spiritual substance of the liturgy is the presence and activity of Jesus Christ.[5] This activity of Christ alone is what makes the human action possible. Through Christ, men, justified and sanctified, are able to approach God, to worship him and offer him sacrifice. Man's activity in worship certainly does have a distinctive importance and high dignity. This applies both to the actions of the liturgical minister and to those of the congregation. But this activity is made possible solely by Christ's work for men. Such a viewpoint throws light upon the dialectical sense of the term "divine service". The word has in fact a double meaning. It signifies God's service to man and, also, man's service to God. To have a complete notion of what happens in worship we must keep both aspects in mind; and the proper order must be preserved. Otherwise a false piety emerges, a piety not in conformity with faith. A correct view of the liturgy removes from man any shadow of false and self-

[5] Cf. *Const.*, art. 7.

righteous piety.[6] It gives him true humility so that he does not impute to himself what is the work of God towards him. But this by no means deprives man of the power and desire to act. It gives him, rather, for the first time, the supreme opportunity of doing so. The believer who is brought up to regard the liturgy in this way lives by the humble and joyful certainty that he shares in redemption through the worship of the Church. This creates a consciousness of which the youth of today stand in great need, the consciousness that participation in the liturgical life of the Church is not primarily a duty, but a favour, not a burden, but a gift. This does not mean that the obligation inherent in the concept of worship should be removed or regarded as secondary. Participation in public worship is a duty as well. But it matters a lot to religion whether instruction about participation in worship is entirely, or almost entirely, dominated by the thought of duty, or is pervaded with the thought of the joy we have at meeting Christ and his work in the life of the Church.

Can simple people and youth make sense of the essence of the liturgy as we have explained it, or is that too difficult for them? The difficulty lies not in the subject but in the method. This view of the liturgy must be presented through popular instruction. It must not, therefore, be conveyed in the abstract manner of technical theological language. If

---

[6] Cf. *Const.* art. 10; also arts. 8, 9 where a further dimension of the liturgy is emphasized.

it is presented in concrete, pictorial language, simple Christians will understand it.[7]

A Catholic Catechism[8] states this truth about the essence of the liturgy as the foundation of all teaching on the sacraments. In section 53—*The Church Celebrates the Worship of God*—it affirms: "When we come together for the Church's worship, Christ is present in our midst . . . Because Jesus is our High Priest we pray and offer 'through Christ our Lord'." Section 54 —*The Church Administers the Holy Sacraments*—expands this idea: "In the sacraments it is Christ our High Priest who is at work . . . Christ distributes to us through the sacraments the graces which he has won for us on the cross."

The new German Catechism is not content with teaching about the various sacraments separately. Before dealing with the separate sacraments it conveys a unified Christological picture of the Church's worship. In this way it fulfils one condition of true liturgical instruction. The fact that the Catechism presents this doctrine of the essence of the liturgy also proves that this is no pet idea of those obsessed with the liturgy. This is part of the Church's treasure of faith which is to be taught to the young, and not just if the teacher happens to feel like it. Finally the Catechism proves that this truth can be conveyed in popular speech which the young can understand.

[7] Cf. *Const.* art. 11.

[8] Burns & Oates, London, 1958—hereafter referred to as "the new German Catechism".

IV

THE PURPOSE OF THE LITURGY

THE liturgy is a purposeful thing aiming at an end. What is it all about? Because the liturgy in its essence is the priestly action of Christ and the Church, the question can be put more precisely: what is the object of this priestly activity?

The incarnation of the Son of God had a double aim: the glorifying of God, and the redemption of the world. The function of his earthly life was to attain this end. This was the will of the Father which the Son had to fulfil. Christ's continuing work in the Church has no other aim. Christ lives and works in the Church for the sake of God's glory and the sanctification of man.

The Church shares in this function and this aim. The purpose of the Church's activity, therefore, has to do with the glorifying of God and the sanctification of man. Because this work of Christ and the Church is accomplished supremely in the liturgy, we can designate this twofold activity as the object of the liturgy.

The rule of God through the liturgy

In technical theological language the two purposes of this twofold aim are described as the *latreutic* and the *soteriological*. To express these two aspects in terms of the history of redemption we must make use of the central biblical concept of the kingdom of God. The kingdom of God is nothing else than the rule of God which has come to men and is constantly coming to men in Christ. Wherever this rule is established, however, there God is glorified; for there God is recognized as lord and king of all. The salvation of the creature is indissolubly bound up with the rule of God. Wherever this rule impinges upon man, man's salvation – his *health* – begins; deliverance and elevation of man takes place. By accepting the rule of God, man enters into eternal life and eternal salvation.

The kingdom of God was not merely a topic of the preaching, but was embodied in the whole activity of Christ. Christ not only preached the kingdom of God: he brought it as well. In his life and work the rule of God was already inaugurated. "If I by the Spirit of God cast out devils," he could say, "then is the kingdom of God come upon you" (Mt. 12:28).

True, this is but the beginning, not the consummation of the kingdom. That will only come about through the return of Christ and will consist in the final victory over the power of Satan and the manifest establishment of the rule of God throughout all creation.

Christ continues to work in his Church, that is, in her and through her Christ is building up the kingdom of God during the period between his first and second coming. This is effected through the Church's activity as a whole, but principally through preaching and the celebration of public worship. The Church has no other message to preach than the message Christ her Lord preached: the good news of the coming of the royal rule of God. But just as Christ did not merely preach this kingdom but really brought it about, so the Church's function is not confined to speaking about the rule of God but assists its actual establishment. It is in the sacraments above all that the rule of God comes to men; for the redemptive activity of Christ really and truly comes to men through them, and the object of that activity is the onset of the kingdom of God.[1]

The reality of the kingdom of God is one of the leading thoughts in the German Catechism (cf. sections 3, 22, 135, 136). This thought is stressed in the doctrine of the sacraments by making the basic introductory text in the two most important sacraments, Baptism and Holy Eucharist, show the relationship of these sacraments to the kingdom of God. Thus the sacraments are integrated in the whole scheme of redemption.

Even the sacramentals assist in the establishment of the rule of God. The fact that the Church consecrates and blesses people and things by prayer and imposition of hands presupposes that people and

[1] What this means for the understanding of the separate sacraments has been shown by Michael Schmaus with reference to the sacrament of Penance. Cf. his study: *Reich Gottes und Buss-sakrament* (Munich 1950). What is said there about the initiation of the kingdom of God through this sacrament is typical of all the sacraments. All of the sacraments serve to start up the rule of God.

things stand in danger of falling under the dominion of evil. By its consecrations and blessings the Church desires to deliver all things – men, cattle, homes and steadings, food and clothing, tools, machines, implements – from the disintegrating power of evil, and subject them to the rule of God. Thus the sacramentals must not be regarded merely as things which bring advantages to men and protect men from harm. Admittedly that is one of their functions; they promote the well-being of men, of animals, of things. But this is neither their only nor even their primary function. They, too, are signs and instruments of the emerging kingdom of God. And so the new Catechism also teaches in section 55: "The sacramentals are there to help us to live a holy life in this world and to use things for the glory of God and our own salvation."

What has been said of the sacraments and of sacramentals applies in like manner to the Church's Divine Office as well. A very definite characteristic feature of the Divine Office is that the thought of giving glory to God is specially stressed. The Divine Office is, as a rule, more thoroughly imbued with worship, praise, and adoration of God than private prayer is. We need only point to the psalms which testify in countless places to the truth of God's sovereignty and rule, and which constitute by far the biggest part of the Divine Office.

To sum up: through the public worship of the Church, Christ is establishing the rule of God upon this earth in the period between his first and second coming. That is to say: the eternal kingdom of God comes to men through the public worship of the Church.

The liturgy and the history of redemption

What significance has it for liturgical instruction if we see the liturgical life of the Church within the setting of the kingdom of God?

When speaking of the essence of the liturgy we discussed the importance of an over-all picture of the liturgy. By gaining insight into the essence of the liturgy, the believer sees worship as a unified reality, an interconnected whole. This comprehensive picture is expanded still further by reflecting on the meaning and aim of the liturgy. We have seen that it is the function of the liturgy to be the place where the rule of God breaks in upon life. The liturgy shares this function in common with the other spheres of Church life. All of the Church's life subserves this great and sacred aim. The Church is the chosen place for the coming of God's rule. To see worship in the light of the kingdom of God is to see it as part of the whole life of the Church. Thus the liturgy is not a self-contained, isolated and enclosed area within the Church. Worship does not then exist alongside preaching and the pastoral office in the Church, dis-related and foreign to them. On the contrary, it appears as integrated within the total image of the Church. In this way its meaning and warrant is understood better and more deeply. Thus the survey over worship is extended to take in the whole Church.

But the concept of God's rule in terms of the history of redemption sets the liturgy within an even wider context. Relationships spread out even farther afield.

Because the whole of the history of redemption from creation until the restoration of the world is the story of the warfare, the victory, the inauguration and the consummation of God's rule, therefore the liturgy of the Church, too, has its place in this mighty process. It is only when he sees it within this complete conspectus that the believer recognizes the whole meaning, greatness, and importance of the Church's worship. The worship of the Church is an integrant component of the whole of redemptive history. At its heart all of human history is *redemptive history*, the story of the redemption of men and of the world. It begins with the creation of man; it follows its course through the Fall and the redemption to its consummation in the new world of eternity which is nothing other than the perfect kingdom of God. In the light of the truth of the kingdom of God, the believer thus sees the whole reality of human history and the world as one huge inter-related whole. Public worship, too, is integrated within this total picture, when seen in the light of the kingdom of God. In this way the utmost limit of what is possible by way of a total over-all picture is achieved.

Reverting once again to St. Thomas's assertion that part of a complete education consists in having a comprehensive view of the whole of reality and seeing the separate spheres integrated within the whole, we may say that the truth of the kingdom of God has given us this comprehensive view of all things and this integration of all the separate parts. And if in addition we recall St. Augustine's saying that the whole gives more delight than the parts, we may add that this integration of worship within the totality of the history of redemption is able to release a great and deep joy in the beholder, and that it can represent a powerfully effective force in education.

V

GIVING GLORY TO GOD

SEEN from the standpoint of the history of redemption the whole idea of the liturgy is the coming of God's sovereign rule to men. The biblical message of the rule or kingdom of God expresses all those things that we have still to expound in detail: the theocentric, the Christocentric, the ecclesiological, and the anthropocentric elements in Christian worship. In brief, the kingdom of God is the rule of God which comes to men. This is not an idea but the reality of the living God who establishes his rule amongst men. Wherever this rule is accepted by men God is glorified as the absolute and the only Lord. The kingdom of God comes through Christ. It cannot be separated from him. No one can enter the kingdom of God and by-pass Christ. Entry is possible through faith in him. The coming of the kingdom of the Father through the Son in the power of the Holy Spirit is realized supremely in the liturgy of the Church. If a man accepts the kingdom of God it means first of all that he has found his true Lord and has been delivered from bondage to the false lord. And then it means that he is re-born into a new eternal life of union with God. For man this life is *eternal salvation*, unsurpassable, eternal fulfilment and perfection.

The biblical concept of the kingdom of God ex-

66

presses, therefore, the twofold meaning of the liturgy: glory to God, and the perfection of man.

First let us turn to the theocentric factor in this activity. The question is: how is God glorified in the liturgy, and what tasks does this set liturgical education?

The theocentric structure of the liturgy

As we saw, the papal encyclical *Mediator Dei* defined the liturgy as the public worship offered to the Father by Christ and the faithful. It is striking how much the encyclical stresses the glory of God as the primary purpose of the liturgy. This is expressly stated frequently and with emphasis.[1] Accordingly the liturgy is meant primarily to give glory to God. This theocentric structure of the liturgy is founded deep in the nature of God and of man. As creator God is absolute Lord of mankind. The only reasonable response by man, because it is the only response that corresponds to reality, is the voluntary recognition of the sovereignty of God. This recognition constitutes the core of adoration and giving glory to God, and is the supreme function of man. This function is inherent in his nature as a creature endowed with freedom. By original sin man denied God this recognition and glory, and at the same time missed the true meaning of his own life. Henceforth

[1] *Christian Worship*, London, Catholic Truth Society, 1947.

man was no longer capable in himself of giving honour to God in full measure. Not until Christ offered it did God once again receive the glory to which he was entitled. Christ's whole life was a constant performance of this glorifying through his utter surrender to the will of his Father. He could say: "My meat is to do the will of him that sent me" (John 4:34). The climax of this glorifying came with the sacrifice of his life on the Cross.

In his Church Christ perpetuates this work of giving glory to the Father. This he achieves by the preaching of his word which is, in fact, the message of the advancing kingdom of God; and through the sacraments. Christ is active in all of the sacraments as priest. To be a priest is to serve God and man. First and foremost the priest turns to God and honours him by his devotion in prayer and sacrifice. With Christ it is no different. But because Christ acts in all of the sacraments as priest, he gives glory to God in all of the sacraments. This glorifying reaches its climax in the Eucharist, for it is the actual commemoration of the sacrifice of Christ.

Christ takes the Church with him in his priestly activity. The Church's priesthood is indeed nothing but the sharing in the priesthood of Christ. It is not Christ alone who acts in the sacraments, but Christ and the Church – the whole Church in its hierarchically constituted order – exercise their priesthood in the sacraments. For our present study that means: in the sacraments the Church not only receives and mediates graces, but glorifies God in them. And because like Christ her high-priest she exercises her priesthood in all of the sacraments, she gives honour and glory to God in all of the sacraments.

We find this theocentric order of the Church's life of worship in the sacramentals as well. There, too, Christ's priesthood is at work. When, in her consecrations and blessings, the Church makes petition to God, she does so "per Dominum nostrum", through our Lord. This priestly activity of the Church, too, is a sharing in the priesthood of Christ. It is of another kind from the priestly activity of the sacraments; but because it is a priestly activity, it is directed primarily to the glory of God. Thus, in the relevant sphere, the Church does not ask merely for help for men, for protection against damage and loss, but prays primarily that men will use material things in such a way as to acknowledge and glorify God as Lord of all things. The idea which is uppermost is that our use of material things is a witness to God the Lord. Not least, therefore, the Church beseeches God to bless animals, houses, steadings, food, tools and machines. Although on the surface it might appear that the sacramental prayers are concerned not with the glory of God, but rather with helping man and nothing more, yet the prime, if not always explicitly stated, object is the glorification of God. Even in these prayers God is the ultimate end. The deepest intention behind these prayers is the recognition of God as creator and Lord, as the origin and the end, the guardian and protector of all things.

Because of this, however, supplication for help is

neither set aside nor even undervalued. There is nothing unworthy or despicable in this; but it is necessary that the supplication be made in the proper manner. This is done when a man expresses on the one hand his own impotence and vulnerability, and, on the other, the omnipotence and goodness of God, and when he does not desire to make God serve his own will, but puts himself at the disposal of God's will, so that in his supplications and desires it is not himself but God who is *the Lord*.

The theocentric structure that we discovered in the sacraments and sacramentals is in evidence in liturgical prayer also. It would be impossible to know where to start or where to finish if we began quoting texts from the Divine Office that have to do with the honour and praise of God. Hymns, psalms, and collects are full of it.

The theocentric functions of liturgical education

The theocentric understanding of the liturgy is of great moment not only for liturgical education, but for Christian life in general. For the real task for man consists in glorifying God by his life. Modern thought and the modern attitude to life to a great extent stand in contrast and opposition to this notion of life. The Christian view, or the view of religion in general, which sees God as the determining centre of existence has been superseded since the start of modern times by the idea that man is the centre of

existence, and that he bears within himself the meaning and end of his life. The underlying attitude to
life has been more strongly conditioned by this notion
than has conscious thought; and this fact has not
been without its influence upon the piety of Christian
people. We have touched on this in our discussion on
understanding the essence of the liturgy. This influence has led to a shift of accent. We need not look so
far afield as the radical humanists of the Enlightenment for whom religion was but the best means of
attaining morality, and who saw the chief purpose of
the liturgy as the advancement and improvement of
morals. The piety of Christians is moulded not by
belief alone, but also by that which we call the
attitude to life of a particular era. Hence it is not
surprising if modern anthropocentricism has struck a
sympathetic chord in the life of piety also. This may
be seen at various points in modern piety. It becomes
clear, for example, when we analyse the life of prayer.
That prayer should be first and foremost the praise
and glorifying of God is obviously not denied in
theory. But if we take a look at modern prayer books
it becomes plain how often practice has taken a
different road. The above-mentioned shift of accent
is seen even in the popular conception of the sacraments. The sacraments are seen and valued almost
exclusively in terms of a means of grace. The other
truth that in the sacraments, in *all* of the sacraments,
God is glorified, is scarcely alive. And yet, this is a
central truth without which complete understanding
of the sacraments is impossible. If the theocentric

aspect is neglected, then this has a profound and far-reaching effect upon the piety of the faithful. For example, this neglect may have the result that in receiving the sacrament of Penance a man thinks only of receiving forgiveness of sins, and not of the task of giving glory to God. It may lead further to a man's being no longer able to understand and perform the Eucharistic prayer which is so explicitly a prayer of praise and honour to God. Instead, however, of continuing to analyze further the piety of the faithful, it would be better for us to speak of the tasks which arise from these considerations.

Education in a theocentric concept of existence is one of the basic tasks for Christian education. The place where a man sets the centre of gravity of his life – in God, or in himself – determines the meaning and value of his life. Such instruction is not a task for liturgical education alone, but of Christian education in general. Thus it can be performed only within the framework of total catechetical instruction. It has to be founded upon the doctrine of faith and morals, in the doctrine of God in that it is stressed that God is the Lord of all, from whom man derives his existence and whom he must serve and worship by his whole life. In teaching about Christ he must be shown to be not only redeemer, the bringer of grace, but also the one who restores glory to God, and whose whole life reaches its climax in giving glory to the Father through perfect obedience. The same applies to the teaching about the Holy Spirit, about the Church, and about the commandments, to name but a few specially important topics.

Concerning liturgical education, education in theocentric piety must form part of 1, basic instruction, and 2, the teaching about the separate sacraments.

1. Liturgical education will be mainly undertaken through the Catechism. Section 53 of the new Catechism states the general basis for all liturgical education. What the Church does in her corporate worship is thus described: "In public worship the Church praises and honours God, thanks him for his goodness, offers atonement for sins, and asks him for his gifts." This text describes, then, the fulness of that which the Church does; but first place is given to the glorifying of God that is expressed through adoration, praise, thanksgiving and atonement. A few lines further on the same order of precedence occurs where we read that the glorifying of God and the imparting of grace to men are dependent upon the participation of the individual. And so in this catechetical instruction the adoration of God is taken very seriously as the primary end of all liturgical activity, and is turned into a practical truth. The fact that it is Christ as high priest who is the agent in the public worship of the Church, alone making it possible for the Church to glorify God, is indicated in several places.[2] The doctrine of the priesthood of the Church, general as well as particular, could be developed in connection with this truth, in the spirit of theocentric education.

[2] Cf., say, sections 47, 53, 54.

2. Because in every sacrament and in every sacramental, first and foremost God is being glorified, instruction on the various sacraments and sacramentals must also pay heed to this theocentric factor. Hence instruction must not speak only of that which we men receive from the sacraments. This is particularly important with regard to instruction about the Holy Eucharist. The Eucharist is the sacrifice of Christ and the Church. The sacrifice of Christ: because Christ gives glory to the Father by his self-oblation. The sacrifice of the Church: because the whole Church gives glory to the Father through an oblation of which it is made capable by Christ. If our instruction on the Eucharist is not to become one-sided, these truths must be kept in mind. In its doctrine of Christ the Catechism already treats of Christ's sacrifice in this spirit.[3] The same tendency is expressed in several places, and with special emphasis in the doctrine of the Eucharist. Thus section 77 contains the following sentences: "In the holy sacrifice of the Mass Christ gives us a share in his sacrifice on the Cross. He incorporates us in his oblation to the Father . . . Through the Holy Eucharist the greatest possible glory and thanksgiving is offered to God." In order to apply these basic truths to the life of the individual the context provides the following sentence: "In the holy Mass I will completely offer myself, along with him (Christ), to the Father."[4] Subsequently this line of thought is continued in the

[3] Cf. section 32, especially questions 55 and 57.
[4] Section 77; cf. section 76.

explanation of the separate parts of the Mass.[5]

In the Catechism there are numerous points of departure for an education leading to the glorifying of God. These are to be found in the doctrine of the Eucharist and also in the instruction on the other sacraments and on the sacramentals and on prayer. Thus the first section formulates the duty of the baptized in a sentence from St. Ignatius of Loyola: "Man has been created to praise God his Lord, to honour and to serve him, and so to save his own soul." The doctrine of prayer unequivocally stresses the idea of the glorifying of God as the determining principle of prayer (cf. sections 70-2). These opportunities are only selected as a few examples.

This question of the theocentric character of the liturgy is concerned with no mere theoretical knowledge, but with a truth that should determine the actual life of the Church and her members in a fundamental and a very practical fashion.

[5] Cf. section 79, under the sub-division: *What we must know concerning the celebration of holy Mass.*

VI

CHRIST AT THE CENTRE OF
THE LITURGY

I T is an essential feature of Christian worship to be
not only theocentric but also Christocentric. The
Christocentric aspect does not, however, compete
with the theocentric, but is an essential and necessary
part of it. For the path of the Father to mankind runs
through the incarnate Son, and man's approach to
the Father opens up only through him who described
himself as "the way" (John 14:6). In this
sense, therefore, the incarnate Word stands in the
centre. Christ is the mediator between God and
man.

This is what we mean by "Christocentric". In this
sense the word does not affirm that Christ is the
ultimate goal of faith. This ultimate goal is the
Father. The word "theocentric" means that God the
Father is the origin and the ultimate end: "Christocentric" means that Christ is sole mediator – he
stands in the middle, between God and man. Christ
realizes this mediatorial function in a special way in
the liturgy. In the liturgy he brings the rule and the
grace of God to men, and leads men towards self-
oblation to God. This mediatorial activity of Christ
forms the core of every liturgical action. Thus in its
essence the liturgy is Christocentric.

The Christocentric structure of the liturgy

How can we speak more precisely of the Christo-centric structure of the liturgy? The liturgy bears a fourfold relationship to Christ.

1. Christ is the sacrament behind all sacraments. Jesus Christ is the manifestation of God in human form. In him the invisible God has become visible. Not only so, but in him God has utterly united himself to a human life. He is God-man, a unity of divine and human – hence also material – reality.

This, then, is the nature of a sacrament in general. The peculiarity of a sacrament consists in its being a unity of invisible, divine grace and visible, earthly reality. It is true that between Christ and a sacrament there is an essential and irremovable difference. In Jesus Christ God and man have become one so that we call him the God-man. The sacrament does not attain such a unity. But in spite of the difference there remains enough likeness to justify the comparison. In Christ as in the sacraments we meet a unity of invisible, divine and visible, earthly reality.

There exists, therefore, an essential connection between Christ and the sacraments. The sacraments do not stand in contradiction to so-called *pure* or *true* Christianity. On the contrary they are so much part of the full reality of Christ that without them the Christian faith would be a headless corpse.

2. The connection between Christ and the sacra-ments is also founded upon the express intention and will of Christ. Christ instituted the sacraments. Not

upon their own initiative but following his command did the disciples baptize: "Going, therefore, teach ye all nations; baptizing them in the name of the Father and of the Son and of the Holy Ghost. And behold, I am with you all days, even to the consummation of the world" (Mt. 28:19 f). According to this there subsists not just an essential, but an historical connection, too, between Christ and the sacraments. Christ is the sacrament behind all sacraments, and the author of the sacraments.

3. The relationship is deeper yet. In every sacrament Christ is the *minister principalis*. The human administrator is the *minister secundarius*, "the second servant". Thus the sacraments are not just performed by the Church at Christ's command; Christ himself performs them through his Church. No sacrament can be separated from Christ. "In the whole conduct of the liturgy," says the encyclical *Mediator Dei*, "the Church has her divine Founder present with her."[1]

4. The grace mediated through the sacraments must also be seen in close and essential relation to Christ. They consist, in fact, in sharing in the life of Christ himself. This is true of the Eucharist in a greater degree than of any other sacrament. In this sacrament the believer receives the body and blood of Christ himself. But the grace mediated by the other sacraments likewise signifies a sharing in Christ. The baptized, for example, receives not only forgive-

[1] *Christian Worship*, London, Catholic Truth Society, 1947, section 19.

ness of sins, but incorporation into Christ as well. Indeed, it is only through membership in Christ and sharing in his life that he becomes a child or son of God.

It is clear, therefore, that from nature, origin, cause, and effect, the sacraments bear a deep and necessary relationship to Christ. Christ is the institutor of the sacraments, but not in the sense that having once instituted them he then withdrew from them. Christ is the type of all sacraments, but not in the sense that he operates as an ideal existing somewhere or other. The institutor, who is also the type, is active as priest in the sacraments through which he grants his faithful a share in his own life. Consequently, the sacraments not only cannot be understood apart from Christ; but Christ is the real and living centre of the sacraments. To sum up: the liturgy possesses a Christocentric structure.

The problem of Christocentric instruction

Liturgical instruction must include the fulness of Christ's relationship with the sacraments. Consequently all four of these relationships must be the subject of instruction. The new Catechism provides good opportunity for this. We must anticipate the objection that the first relationship – Christ as the sacrament behind all sacraments – is not explicitly stated in the Catechism. This would normally be too difficult a concept for children. But in the top grades of the secondary school and in religious classes for adolescents the idea can and ought to be taken up. It is good, if it can be explained; for by presenting Christ as the type of all sacraments something very significant can be accomplished. Presumably it is not only amongst intellectuals that the idea that the sacraments and sacramentals are things strange, even opposed, to the Christian faith is more widely disseminated than those within the Church generally admit. If in opposition to this the truth is taught that Christ is the type of the sacraments, then the foundation is laid for a radically different and quite new mentality. In this way not only will the idea that there is an opposition between the Christian faith and sacraments be exposed as a misunderstanding which neglects essential features in the figure of Christ; but in this way we will be able to lay the foundation for a believing understanding of the sacraments, that reveals them as an integrant part of the whole Christ-event. Knowledge of these interconnections is indispensable for a conscious and mature faith.

A peculiarity of the German Catechism of 1955 is that the Christological truths exercise a determining influence on doctrine as a whole. This is specially true of the doctrine of the Church and of the last things. The influence is even stronger upon the instruction about the sacraments.

Whereas the Catechism of Joseph Deharbe – dominant since the middle of last century – even in its 1925 revision by Th. Monnich – known as the *Unity Catechism* – saw the relationship between Christ and the sacraments almost exclusively in terms of their institution, the Catechism of 1955 presents deeper features: Christ is now represented as author and as *minister principalis* of every sacrament; and the grace obtained through Christ is also described, amongst other ways, in terms of a sharing in the life of Christ.

The Christocentric viewpoint is attained chiefly by Christ being described, both in the foundation of the doctrine of the sacraments, and in the separate sections on the sacraments, as the principal administrator. In the two basic sections on the liturgy (53 and 54) this priestly action of Christ is affirmed with unmistakable clarity. Section 53 runs: "When we are assembled for worship Christ is in our midst. He is our high-priest; the priest at the altar is merely his representative. Because Christ is our high priest, we pray and sacrifice through Jesus Christ our Lord." Section 54 expands this statement: "In the sacraments it is Christ our high priest who is at work . . . In the sacraments Christ gives us grace . . ." Finally, we add the significant and beautiful words of section 47: "The congregation, assembled for worship, are holy: they are the people of God; Christ is in their midst; they are filled with the Holy Spirit."

This Christocentric understanding is applied to every sacrament. Characteristic of this is the alteration in the formulation of the questions about the effect of the various sacraments. In the earlier *Unity*

Catechism we read, for example, the following text: "What does Confirmation effect? Confirmation imparts the Holy Spirit to us so that we may confess the faith steadfastly, and persevere in withstanding the enemy of our salvation." By contrast, the new Catechism puts it thus: "What does Christ effect in Confirmation? In Confirmation Christ fills us with the Holy Spirit so that we may steadfastly confess the faith, fight bravely against the enemy of our salvation and help on the work of sanctifying the world" (question 139). The formula undergoes a corresponding alteration for all the sacraments.

The emphatic insistence on the active presence of the glorified Lord is to be found even apart from the answers to the questions. It is seen frequently in the expository texts concerning the sacraments, rightly accentuated with special force in the sacrament of Penance. A few sentences from the section: *The Sacrament of Penance* (84), show the consistency with which the Christocentric theme is followed out. "In his love Christ comes to help the sinner through a special sacrament . . . in Confession Christ helps us . . . when the priest gives us absolution Christ our redeemer forgives us our sins . . . reconciles us with his heavenly Father . . . gives us back the life of grace . . . he increases the life of grace in us, and gives us fresh strength not to sin again."

The reality of the active presence of Christ in the liturgy is like a light shining upon every sacrament. This light radiates out from the hidden centre of the mysteries.

The Christocentric view of the sacraments is deepened and enriched by teaching the idea, already mentioned, that the grace mediated by the sacraments signifies incorporation in Christ and sharing in his life, although this may not be the only or even the primary significance.[2]

The Christocentric meaning of liturgical life is noticeable also in the teaching on the Christian Year. Sunday, for example, is no longer celebrated primarily in Old Testament terms as the day of rest and the day of creation, but as the day of Christ and of the new creation begun in his Resurrection.[3]

What does understanding the liturgy Christocentrically mean?

1. By a Christocentric understanding the liturgy is drawn into the redemptive work of Christ. In this way its dependence upon and orientation towards Christ is seen as of its nature, and as necessary. This representation of the liturgy makes it no longer possible to think of the sacraments as things opposed to the intention of the author of the Christian religion. Rather the reverse is what we experience, that whoever believes in Christ has to accept the liturgy at least in essence. It is impossible, on this view, to conceive of the Church as the Church of the Word alone. Such a one-sided conception would exclude a vital sphere of Christ's activity. The Christocentric instruction on the mysteries of the Church brings to

[2] Cf., say, The doctrine of Baptism (section 63).
[3] Cf. sections 103 and 105; cf. also *Const.*, art. 102.

the faithful the knowledge that the sacramental life derives its justification and meaning from faith in Christ.

2. It follows, too, from the Christocentric view that the faithful look upon the whole liturgy as a huge, unified reality, as the presence of the glorified Lord in his mysteries. In speaking of the essence of the liturgy we have already dealt with this. Let us take note, however, of another result.

Through this viewpoint the function of the human agent in the sacraments for the first time receives a true appraisal. This function becomes clearly and explicitly characterized as instrumental: "In the sacraments it is Christ our high priest who is at work; the men who administer the sacraments are his instruments" (section 54). What an increase in conscious and joyful readiness to share in the sacramental life of the Church might be achieved by a pastoral leadership which knew how to exploit the truth that it is *Christ* who acts upon us in every sacrament through the human dispenser! The function of the human agent, which, since the Counter Reformation, in sermons and instruction, has frequently been stressed beyond due bounds, even exaggerated, would thus be restored to its proper, theologically based, pedagogically sound perspective, in favour of the importance of the *minister primarius*. This would by no means result in a minimizing of the status of the *minister secundarius*. On the contrary the dignity of the human dispenser would only then be seen in its true brightness.

In giving instruction on the sacraments, whether I speak only of the human minister, or speak explicitly of Christ as the invisible but most important minister, is clearly of the greatest moment. It must surely be obvious that we would win the hearts of children and youth for the sacraments to a very much greater extent if we gave preference to the second rather than to the first type of instruction. The type of instruction must not, however, be left to subjective whim.

3. Finally, let us mention a third point arising from the Christocentric structure of the liturgy. On this view, the person of the Redeemer himself stands at the centre of sacramental activity. At the centre, that is, there stands a concrete and perceptible figure. In the sacraments it is not the mystery of the invisible God, but God made visible who meets the faithful; and, moreover, it is not just any figure, but that one whom the faithful obey, honour and love as they do no other.

The faithful must be trained to find Christ present and active in the sacraments; but this concept is, unfortunately, not a common possession amongst our church-going people. The consciousness of the presence of Christ is largely confined to his presence in the tabernacle. That it is Christ who dispenses grace in Baptism, Penance, Anointing of the Sick, and in the rest of the sacraments, is not part of the common inheritance of living faith. All the more urgent, then, is the work of preaching and education.

VII

THE LITURGY AS THE PUBLIC WORSHIP OF THE CHURCH

THERE can be nothing upon which representatives of the liturgical revival all over the world are so united as the demand that the liturgy should once again become the public worship of the whole Church. On every side, no truth is so much recognized as the fact that the liturgy is something for all of the faithful and not for the clergy alone. Everywhere it is stressed that the liturgy should be celebrated by the whole people. In this there is no neglect of the authority and importance of the office-bearers of the Church, but what is indicated is that all who have been made members in the people of God through Baptism should take part in the celebration. From this truth alone are drawn the numerous practical consequences of this sort in the field of the arrangement of worship. This is the aspect that the revival of worship has pushed most forcibly to the fore. The leaders of the Church themselves have applauded this new evaluation of the corporate character of the liturgy. The encyclical *Mediator Dei* asserts that: "Another advantage of the movement has been to call special attention to the doctrine that all the faithful form one closely-knit body of which Christ is the Head, and that it is the duty of the Christian people to take its appointed part in the liturgy."[1] This text, that is, affirms the fact that all the faithful make up a community as closely-knit as the members of a human body. Second, from this fact the inference is drawn that it is a duty of the faithful to play their appropriate part in the liturgy. This is most worthy of note; for in the technical literature of the last few centuries this view was not the dominant one. That literature frequently stressed the opposite, that the liturgy was an action of the clergy, of the ordained. Consequently the part of the faithful was as a rule simply ignored or touched on only peripherally.

Before coming to deal with the practical problems of liturgical education that arise from the corporate character of the liturgy we must first clarify the essential features of this corporate character of the liturgy.

The liturgy is the public worship of the people of God

The nature of the Church is described in two biblical images: the image of the human body, and the image of a people. The Church is the mystical body of Christ, and the people of God. Both images represent the Church as a community. A body is a unity of many members, and a people is a community of men. The Church is not the sum of many individuals, each one existing for himself alone. In its

[1] *Christian Worship*, London, Catholic Truth Society, 1947, section 5; cf. *Const.* arts. 14, 26, 28, 30, 31, 50-54.

essence it is a community. It is the *ecclesia*, the assembly of those called by God through Christ. Furthermore, the images of body and people embody the fact that the Church is a body, the members of which are not all alike, but have various functions. Each member in any body has its specific function. Each member is important for the body as a whole, but all the functions are different. A people, too, is a community, articulated and stratified. All citizens do not discharge the same function for the whole community. In the Church it is not otherwise.

The Church is composed of members who bear the general priesthood, and of members who in addition have received a special priesthood.[2] The special priesthood does not stand in opposition to the general priesthood and to the community. On the contrary it is there for the very purpose of building up the community of the Church. The name "orders" expresses this social function of the special priesthood, the official priesthood.

The Church is thus a hierarchically graded community. The Church as this community is, along with Christ, the bearer of the liturgy. In this way we reject the one-sided notion that makes it appear as though only the official priesthood were the bearers of the liturgy. It is the Church in its totality, in the unity and diversity of its members, that celebrates the liturgy. For our study that is the first and basic fact.

The second fact does not limit the first, but com-

[2] Cf. *Const.*, art. 14.

pletes and interprets it. The second fact arises from
the assertion, just made, that the Church is a hierarchically ordered community in which the members
have different powers and functions. For the celebration of the liturgy this means that all cannot do
everything. The unordained faithful do not possess
the powers possessed by those in orders. The fact that
those in official priestly orders have been endowed
with special power has often been taught during the
last few centuries in a one-sided way, to the detriment of the rights and functions of the general
priesthood. This can be understood as a reaction to
the thesis of the Reformers that there is only a
priesthood of all believers. Today there is no longer a
danger of being misunderstood when we describe the
greatness and dignity of the priesthood of all the
baptized, and the function which this implies. Now it
is time to teach clearly the truth that the laity are
not mere objects but subjects also of public worship.
This is not to obscure the authority and prestige of
those in office, but brings clearly into the light once
again the all too long forgotten dignity of all the
members of the Church. It is not Catholic to teach
only the priesthood of all believers; but in justice we
must add immediately that neither is it Catholic to
speak *only* of the special priesthood. It is Catholic to
see and to teach the whole fulness of the priestly life
within the Church. This fulness, however, is presented
only through both forms of the priesthood; and both
are nothing else than a sharing in the priesthood
of Christ.

*The social structure of the liturgy
under the aspect of education*

The sacraments impart grace to the individual, and in every sacrament the individual meets God. An individual dispenses, and an individual receives a sacrament.

This truth that a sacrament is the place of meeting between God and the individual has been taken up with special delight by modern piety, the roots of which go back to the Middle Ages. Its mark is clearly upon the popular notion of the sacraments even today. On the other hand, the complementary truth, that each sacrament bears an essential relation to the community, recedes far too much. For example, how many of the faithful know what relation Baptism has to the community of the Church? How many have a keen conception that the reception of the sacrament of Penance likewise is of great moment for the community of the Church? The sense of community is still most commonly found with regard to the Mass; but, on the other hand, even here, the widespread individualistic notion of the sacrament is still in evidence. One need only look on at a so-called parish Mass from the back of the church and observe what the individual worshippers do in the course of the celebration. One may perhaps be surprised at the great number who do not join in the prayers and singing. For the most part this is not because of indifference, because of people wanting merely to "assist" at Mass; it is rather that they are praying their private prayers from some prayer book or other during the common prayer and singing, even while the Word of God is being read out. It is revealing to discover that the faithful do not behave thus during devotions. At devotions of whatever kind, as a rule all of the congregation join in the prayers. On the other hand, at the celebration of the Mass, the mystery of unity and the most important worship of all, people are quick to shut themselves off from the corporate action without a qualm. The individualistic conception is seen today in its crassest form with regard to Communion. Communion is thought of predominantly or even exclusively as the meeting of the individual soul with Christ. The thought that it also signifies union and fellowship with the other members of the Church does not seem to have made much impact.

The examples cited show that in this field liturgical education has serious problems to solve. It has to form the mind of the faithful, especially of the children and youth, in such a way that the one-sided individualistic view of the sacraments is corrected. This must not be accomplished, however, by falling into the opposite extreme and speaking from now on only of the community aspect. Both aspects must be taught in due measure, the community aspect and the individual aspect. But because the community aspect has been so little considered in the past, it has to be specially stressed now. This can best be done through the doctrine of the general priesthood. The saying of St. Peter the apostle about the royal priesthood of all believers in 1 Peter 2:9 is a message worth rediscovering and preaching afresh. It must be touched on in connection with the doctrine of Baptism; for this priesthood is founded upon Baptism. Through Baptism a man becomes a member of the priestly people of God, that is of the Church. He is incorporated in Christ the high priest and in his body. Hence it must not be taught of Baptism merely that it confers forgiveness of sins and makes a man a child of God. Besides this the fact must be stated that a man becomes a member of the people of God and that from henceforth a man must serve God in this community. The doctrine of the priesthood of all believers must be re-affirmed at Confirmation; for in this sacrament it is strengthened and deepened. In Confirmation the fulness of the Spirit is given. The Spirit of God is, however, a Spirit of unity and of fellowship; it is no Spirit of isolation and of living unto oneself. The fulness of the Spirit thus turns the recipient towards the even greater and deeper association with all the members, and demands of him an even greater unselfish service. Furthermore it is important in liturgical education that instruction on the sacrament of Penance should not ignore the relationship to the community. In the human priest the penitent meets not only Christ, but the community of the faithful as well. Sin involves not only guilt in the sight of God; it is also a trespass, an injustice, against the community. For, as every sick member weakens the body, so a sinful member in the body of the Church damages the Church. In the sacrament of Penance the penitent confesses this guilt, and the Church reconciles him with itself through the priest. This concept of Penance can be illustrated by reference to so-called public scandal in which this idea is explicitly stated. The Confiteor in the Mass or in Compline expresses the idea also. Here one confesses one's sin not only to God but to the whole company of the saints – saints of the old and the new Covenants, the members of the Church who are present, and even the angels – and asks for their intercession with God.

Instruction on the sacrament of Holy Matrimony, too, ought to pay heed to the truth of the priesthood of all believers. The fact that it is not the priest present, but the couple themselves who administer this sacrament has always been well-known. In school and especially in pre-marriage instruction it ought, therefore, to be taught also that the couple administer this sacrament by virtue of their priesthood, and that by the exercise of this priesthood they are assisting in the building up of the body of Christ.

Finally, for no sacrament is the truth of the general priesthood so important as for the Eucharist; for it is only by virtue of the priesthood received in Baptism that the faithful are called and enabled to join in the sacrifice. In sections 87 to 96 the encyclical *Mediator Dei* develops the thought of this calling of the faithful. It is true that only the ordained priest by the Consecration makes Christ's sacrifice present. More precisely: Christ makes his sacrifice present through him. And yet the faithful all share in this sacrifice, to such a high degree, that the encyclical says that they present the sacrifice, not just through the priest, but with him, "una cum ipso" (91), so that Christ makes a sacrifice to his Father, along with all his members (92). In this sense the Eucharist is the sacrifice of the whole Church. The celebration of the Mass must be shown to be a community celebration in terms of this central action. No liturgical celebration has so much the appearance of an *assembly* as the Eucharist. The texts and actions of the Mass bear incontestable witness to this structure. Because this idea has become so heavily overshadowed in the piety of the faithful by an individualist view, preaching about the Mass must lay special stress on the community aspect. We must do all in our power to give the celebration of the Mass the form of a communal act. How can a congregation feel itself to be a living society if it does not feel this in the corporate celebration of the Eucharist? According to St. Augustine the Eucharist is the sacrament of unity. It cannot be denied that much has been done by clergy and people in the past decades to make the Mass once again a "sacramentum unitatis". But it is equally undeniable that we have not yet reached the goal, but are still only on our way.

The social structure of the liturgy presents urgent problems not only to education but also for the shaping of the liturgy. The field that opens up here is admittedly so wide that it would be impossible to describe the tasks arising with reference to the separate sacraments and sacramentals. As with the

Eucharist so with all the other liturgical celebrations and ceremonies, we are faced from time to time with the twofold task of instruction and of re-shaping. It would be an equally impossible task to show in detail how much the Catechism teaches about the social side of the Church's public worship. The basic sentence of section 53, already quoted more than once, may be taken as typical of all the liturgical catechesis: "The faithful are to share in public worship by joining in the prayers and in the sacrifice; they have been called and empowered to do this in Baptism. The more perfectly the individual takes part, all the more is God glorified, and all the more grace do all receive from him."

VIII

WORSHIP AS THE WAY
OF LIFE

ANY kind of one-sidedness is foreign to the liturgy. It has a history running into thousands of years. It was not made for individuals nor for an esoteric circle of pious people. Having evolved as the liturgy for the great community of all the faithful, today it is still the public worship of the whole people of God. It would have been doomed to destruction from the start had it been founded upon some special kind of piety. And yet its balanced and measured quality is far removed from mediocrity. Quite the opposite: the liturgy is full of bold and inscrutable thoughts. Even its forms, mostly simple indeed, are yet of great dignity and splendour. Averse to all extremes, the liturgy, which so strongly emphasizes the theocentric factor, grants a place and a fulfilment to legitimate anthropocentric concerns.

The two objectives of worship: the glory of God, and the redemption of man do not stand in opposition. Nor are they even separated from each other, but are essentially integrated. The glorifying of God is bound up with the sanctification fo man, and there is no sanctification apart from honouring God. When man turns to God to praise him, he not only surrenders to God the sovereign Lord, but to God as the boundless fulness and source of life. To turn and surrender to this God of life is to claim a share in "life". This also is true: man only receives grace when he praises and glorifies God. Man cannot take God's grace with one hand and with the other reject God as the Lord. Thus, the glorifying of God and the sanctification of man belong so closely and essentially together that the one cannot exist without the other. Where one is, there is the other as well.

We have already examined the Church's worship under the aspect of the glorifying of God. Now we try to understand it from the point of view of the sanctification of man. What does sharing in the Church's worship mean for the individual?

The texts of the liturgy use many images and concepts to describe what it is that a man receives from the liturgy. This it describes as holiness, justice, freedom, being a child of God, grace, a share in divinity and so on. It is indicated also by a single word, specially meaningful to men today. It speaks frequently of the *life*, that a man receives from public worship. The word "life" appeals directly to every man. Each attaches to it very definite, if various, interests, sorrows, desires, and hopes. The concept of life, as is well-known, plays a dominant role in the literature, philosophy, and theology of our time. It is by no means a new theological concept. It originated in the Bible, and is to be found throughout the tradition of the Church. But in contemporary theology   it   has   acquired   fresh   significance.[1]

The sacraments as mysteries of life

Christ described himself as "the life": "I am the way, the truth, and the life" (John 14:6). He did not say: "I have the life," but "I am the life"; just as he did not say: "I have (or know) the way and the truth," but "I am the way and the truth." He could say this because in his essence he is the Son of God; and God is life and truth in the utmost degree. What that really means escapes our imagination. Life as we know it, earthly life in its various forms, is more unlike than like the life of God. The life of God knows no becoming and no decay. It never *becomes*; it always *is*. It does not originate from nothing and is never threatened by annihilation. It cannot be derived from somewhere else; God possesses it in himself. Consequently it is self-subsistent and of a fulness and power which is immeasurable. We speak of the *unfathomableness* of this life.

Christ has revealed the hidden life of God in order to impart that life to men. This design of revelation is expressly stated in the scriptures of the New Testament. Thus we read at the beginning of the

[1] It is unnecessary to give examples. Let us take note specifically, however, of Michael Pfliegler's book: *Leben, Bildung, Heilige Bildung* ([6]1957), the subject of which is the problem of Christian education from the point of view of life.

first epistle of St. John: "For the life was manifested; and we have seen and do bear witness and declare unto you the life eternal, which was with the Father and hath appeared to us. That which we have seen and have heard, we declare unto you; that you also may have fellowship with us, and our fellowship may be with the Father and with his Son Jesus Christ" (I John 1:2-3; cf. I John 5:11-13; and John 6:40).

Where does man meet this life-giving God? According to the second epistle of Clement (14, 1), a work composed about the middle of the second century by an unknown author, the Church is "the Church of life". The Lord dispenses the new life through his mysteries. There it is offered and shared out to men.

In terms of the divine life mediated through Christ, Baptism is the sacrament of birth into life. Through it a man receives for the first time the new fellowship of life with God. Confirmation strengthens and completes it. It is a favourite device and in accord with ancient theological tradition, to explain the life mediated through Baptism by an analogy with natural life. On this analogy, what happens in Baptism is seen as a birth. Then Confirmation is described as a maturing and as the sacrament of growth. In doing this one is well aware of how this image can be misleading. To grow and mature implies that an already existent life is developing and unfolding from within. But this does not apply to the divine life in man. This life increases by coming down from God *above*. It increases *only* by an infusion from above. This is the only sense in which it grows and matures; and it is in this way that the life implanted through Baptism is strengthened and perfected through Confirmation. The currently used word "Confirmation" meaning *strengthening* or *making firm*, is close in idea to the ancient Christian "perfection".

In the Blessed Sacrament, the sacrament of the Lord's table, we are given "the bread of life".

Sin, by which man separates himself from God, the origin and source of life, causes the death or at least the impairing of this new life. Hence the necessity and reason for the sacrament of Penance. The sacrament of Penance is the mystery of the restoration of lost life, or the healing of impaired life.

The sacrament of Anointing of the Sick signifies that an increase in divine life is being imparted to a man in bodily sickness, at the gates of death. At this point, when the man is acutely aware of the transience and brittleness of his earthly life, he experiences an enrichment of everlasting life.

In Holy Order God increases eternal life by authorizing and equipping the ordained to the special ministry of mediating this life.

Through the sacrament of Holy Matrimony the stream of new life is conducted into the marital life-fellowship of two Christians, to have its effect in this fellowship and in its posterity.

This briefly sketched interpretation shows the sacraments as ways along which eternal life comes to men. To share in celebrating the public worship of the Church means to share in the mysteries of life.

The liturgy as the fulfilment of human life

The importance of this interpretation of Christian worship only becomes completely evident when we contrast it with popular conceptions of the purpose and meaning of the liturgy. Let us make a contrast with reference to two widely held conceptions.

There is a widespread notion that the liturgy of the Church is there to provide civic life with a certain religious embroidery. Even if people no longer go regularly to church themselves, they still persist in having children baptized shortly after they are born. People like to have a church wedding also; for many find a civil wedding too bare and comfortless for their feelings, whereas the solemnizing of the marriage in church lends a certain festive splendour to the affair. Above all people want to have a Christian burial. Should some priest decline – on perfectly legitimate canonical grounds – to allow Christian burial, he almost always provokes a hue and cry. People who have no time for the Church, who may not have taken any part in the life of the Church for years, are enraged if Christian burial is denied some member of their family. People feel that a ceremony in Church is comforting and beneficial. The tone is often set by the still current idea that a decent citizen wants Christian burial, no matter how much a stranger to the Church he may have been.

Alongside this there is another stricter conception of the liturgy: that worship is primarily a matter of duty. Attendance at Sunday Mass is regarded as merely a Sunday duty. One desires to perform a duty and so goes to church. Because devotions or Vespers are not obligatory one need not go to them as well. On this view, attendance at worship is seen as the fulfilment of a duty, as a human service rendered to God. This is a legalistic concept. We go to Mass because the commandment, the law of the Church demands that we go. With this is linked the idea that to miss Mass without excuse is a grave sin meriting eternal punishment, whereas attendance at Mass merits reward. Behind this conception may be a high and strict moral sense. One must guard against despising or ridiculing such a view. It is true that attendance at Sunday Mass is a strict law of the Church. But this conception becomes suspect when it becomes the ruling and perhaps the only powerful conception of the liturgy, when participation in the public worship of the Church is seen only under the aspect of fulfilment of a duty.

The insufficiency of both of the views outlined becomes obvious when we see worship as the imparting of the divine life. What is public worship, seen in that light?

Those who, following the first conception, see public worship only as an adornment of life which satisfies sentiment or civic susceptibilities, take it for granted that the Church's liturgy is something having nothing or little to do with life. It is something solid enough, but has nothing to do with existence. On such a view the liturgy appears as a special, museum-like world that is appealed to on certain festive or sorrowful occasions, but a world that has no point of contact with the real life and interests of men.

A deep and dangerous misunderstanding lies at the bottom of all this. In essence the public worship of the Church is the exact opposite of this notion. Let us admit that worship may be dead and inadequate in its outward form. But consider the core of liturgical action; then the liturgy can provide the fulfilment of human existence. It touches man right in his deepest true and genuine interests. A full life is the embodiment of all a man's desires, the solution of all his problems. Naturally, we men have very different concepts of the life after which we strive. But to hope that one's life will reach its fulfilment is common to all. It is the liturgy that grants men the highest and most intense fulfilment of life. The life it gives transcends all forms and grades of earthly life, and at the same time is of such power and intensity that it represents the unimaginable and unsurpassable fulfilment of all human desires. In its essential content, therefore, the liturgy does not run alongside human life; it does not stand disrelated to the existence of man, apart from his sorrows, fears, and desires. It is not a curiosity for religiously-inclined people. The liturgy is concerned with nothing less than man himself, with the fulfilment of human existence in something eternally valid, to expect which man of himself has neither right nor opportunity. Along with giving glory to God, this fulfilment of human life is precisely the object of public worship. Christ's saying that he has come to give men abundant life (John

10:10) finds its concrete realization for the individual, in the liturgy; for it is Christ himself who applies life to men through the liturgy. Hence the liturgy is no museum full of curious, perhaps very precious, but old-fashioned objects for which modern man has no further use. No matter how much we may seek the cause of this misunderstanding, in the lifeless and unintelligible form of public worship, the opinion, when compared with what really happens in the liturgy, is still a caricature.[2]

The other view, that participation in worship is a mere discharge of duty, can also be corrected at this point. The idea of duty places the human action in the foreground. In these terms, liturgy is primarily a service rendered to God by man. In addition, this action takes on the character of a legal transaction. In reality, however, it is God who is the chief actor in the liturgy. Primarily it is not God who is receiving something here, but man. The new share in his own life, that God offers man through the sacraments, is a gift. It is so much a free gift that man can lay no claim to it whatsoever. It is grace in the original sense: the free gift of the gracious God. Man can do nothing except prepare to receive this gift by faith, love, contrition and penance. Even this preparation, as is well-known, is only possible through the prevenient grace of God. And even the glorifying of God by men in the liturgy is only possible through God's making men capable of it. The sacrifice we offer in the celebration of the Eucharist is given us by God

[2] *Const.*, art. 10.

himself; it is, as the prayer after the account of the institution puts it, "de tuis donis ac datis", of your own gifts. Thus, when man comes to worship he should come in the clear knowledge that he is coming to God in order to receive the great unmerited gift of eternal life. This view will not devaluate the dutiful side of public worship. It will give it a deeper foundation and preserve it from the misunderstanding that public worship is a merely human act.

To understand the liturgy as the way of life is to grasp its urgency. The offer of life through the liturgy faces man with a decision about his eternal salvation. This life has to do, indeed, with the everlasting community of life between man and God, which is nothing other than man's redemption. To reject this offer implies, therefore, rejection of eternal salvation, that is damnation. In this lies the urgency of the liturgy. In the liturgy God confronts man with a decision about his eternal salvation. If a man comes to worship in this spirit and yields himself to the divine action, for him that will mean the utmost intensification of life, and the gaining of eternal redemption. If, on the other hand, he declines to take part in public worship, then he is not only withdrawing from the rule of God, but also robbing himself of the chance of reaching his own eternal goal.

The manner of participation in public worship also bears the stamp of decision. The only proper manner of participating is that of honest self-oblation to God, out of faith and love. The measure of this oblation may influence the measure of grace. The more sincerely a man gives himself up to divine action in the liturgy of the Church, the more abundantly does life flow into him. Indifference and lack of interest are so dangerous precisely because they weaken or even obstruct this stream of life. The attitude of the mere onlooker at Mass is not just stupid; it is dangerous. It rests upon the dangerous error that nothing really happens at public worship. It is an attitude of contempt, or at least of neglect towards the working of God.

To sum up we may say that the liturgy is no optional matter. It is not a more or less beautiful performance that men look at or listen to for their delight, but that does not really concern them. Participation in the liturgy is a mighty, a serious, and also a dangerous affair.

Liturgical instruction as a doctrine of life

If instruction on the liturgy is undertaken in the spirit of this discussion, that is, if it is imparted as a doctrine of life, then it will have far-reaching results for the formation of the mind of the faithful and for the ensuing attitude towards the liturgy. Such instruction only succeeds, it must be admitted, when certain conditions are fulfilled. Preaching on the liturgy, especially on the sacraments, must not, for example, lay the accent upon historical instruction. Historical instruction can be most helpful in liturgical education. Sometimes it is useful to trace back the history of a liturgical action. Many ceremonies become much more intelligible when their origins are known. We need think only of the prayers at the altar steps or of the offertory procession at Mass. The same applies, obviously, to the other sacraments, and to the sacramentals. If we have to speak of Baptism, then, for example, the sealing with the Sign of the Cross can be illustrated by a reference to the ancient custom of branding soldiers and slaves with the sign of their master so that they could henceforth always be recognized as his property. But historical instruction should always be given with an eye to what is the essential substance of the liturgical action. It is of no value in itself. It is of value only as a help in better understanding the contemporary redemptive operation of the liturgy.

Nor must there be a tendency to limit instruction to describing and explaining external actions, gestures, objects. It is important that people should be acquainted with the external, visible ceremonies, above all with the liturgical texts. But as in the liturgy the visible has the function of directing our minds to what is invisible, the presentation of what is external and visible must lead on to the essential, invisible events. This goal is not attained, for example, if one is content to prepare for public worship by practising hymns, even by having the children learn them by heart, in the belief that consequently they will be able to sing them at Mass in the right frame of mind. Even by explaining the substance and the meaning of the words we do not always arrive at what is necessary: an intelligent understanding of the hymns, their content, and relation to the spiritual liturgical action.

From our study so far arises the important demand that liturgical instruction must have as its goal the unlocking of the sacraments as the source of life and redemption. Furthermore, this unlocking must be effected in an *existential* way. What is great, what is ineffable, what is overpowering about this *supernatural* life must be taught so that it is grasped as an *existential* truth. This life must be revealed as the one and only valid salvation, assurance, and consummation of human existence. The goal to strive for would be the creation of a mentality which saw the liturgy and human life not in opposition, but as forming a unity. By instruction, the concept of the liturgy as an island of the blessed, removed from everyday life, must be dispelled. In teaching and training, all that might create the impression that the liturgy is an object for an antiquarian museum must be avoided.

By using the concept of life, instruction becomes concrete. The theological concept of sanctifying grace, for example, may be most useful for precise scientific thought. For popular instruction it is too abstract, as a rule. Who, if he has not had a theological education, can link a concrete image to the phrase "sanctifying grace"? If one uses the phrase in a sermon or in instruction, one has to use pictures to help to elucidate it. All abstract speech is useless in teaching youth and people in general. Such instruction demands picturesque, concrete language. The word "life" is admittedly not perfectly unambiguous; that is its weakness; but those who hear it, be they young or old, immediately associate concrete images with it. These images are full of experiences and meaningful associations. Hence the word "life" immediately says something to a man. In addition it is a dynamic word, whereas sanctifying grace is a static concept. What is dynamic has a more powerful effect on men; they accept it more willingly and more readily allow themselves to be gripped and moved by it.

We are not exaggerating when we say that the concept of life plays a big part in the new German Catechism. The emphatic application of the concept cannot be overlooked. It is one of the characteristic features of this Catechism, and corresponds to the design of the authors to teach the truths of the faith in a manner suited to the sensibilities of modern youth. Decisive and regulative is the understanding of sanctifying grace as a "share in the life of God". Thus the expression "life of grace" is preferred (section 43). Subsequently this interpretation is applied to the doctrine of the sacraments. In section 54 it is said of the sacraments as a whole: "The Church dispenses the seven sacraments so that we may have life and life in abundance." In the same section the sacraments are described as the "fountains of the Redeemer" from which men can draw eternal life (cf. also section 1). The teaching on each separate sacrament follows the same line of thought. A section on Baptism (63) bears the descriptive title: "Baptism is the fountain of new life." The thought that through Baptism Christ grants a share in the divine life is expressed in other places also (1, 34). Of Confirmation, we are taught that by it the life of grace is brought to maturity (74). In the Eucharistic meal, which is a pledge of the banquet of eternal life, the body and blood of the Lord are received as food for eternal life (78). And in the sacrament of Penance as well, the motif of life emerges again, in as much as it is described as the sacrament of the restoration or increase of life through Christ (85). Following this discussion it remains for us to expound the psychological and pedagogical significance of this liturgical doctrine of life.

IX

THE MEETING OF GOD AND MAN

The danger of materializing religious life

RELIGIOUS life consists in the personal fellowship of man with God. It is actualized when man meets God.

To be a person means to subsist in oneself, to have control over oneself, and to stand in relation to other personal beings. In being a person lies the true essence of man, and this essence, which is his fundamental structure, strives for realization. This realization comes about first and foremost in the most varied forms of personal inter-relations. But it is only when the personal *I* attains to a meeting with the absolute *Thou* that it achieves that depth and fulness that it desires. And so the consummation of human life is not attained until man arrives at a personal encounter with God.

From this point of view what does participation in the public worship of the Church mean? Divine service is the public and formal worship of the Church. Is it also the place where the individual meets God? Does the personal being of a man come into its own and find fulfilment in the liturgy?

It does not seem to be so. Not only do contemporary personalist philosophers, but wider circles also, find that the liturgy presents a problem. In this it is not so much isolated acts that are considered doubtful. It is rather the liturgy as such, as an objective religious entity, frozen into externality, that arouses offence and doubts. Truly there is a serious problem here, worth discussing. It would seem that the liturgy necessarily leads to materialization and externalizing of religious life, and that consequently it makes true personal relation difficult if not utterly impossible. The danger appears to be acute in three places.

1. In the liturgy God's action is assured but it happens only if certain specific rituals are carried out. If these are not performed, or not performed properly according to prescription, God does not act. It is argued that this sort of thing implies a limitation of God's freedom to act wherever and whenever he pleases. Because God is thus limited there can be no question of a personal encounter; for such encounter demands freedom to turn to each other.

2. It is thought that the content of the liturgy is what gives rise to the danger of materialization. The content of the liturgy is the grace which is mediated. This concept of the sacraments as means of grace is thought to be a straightforward expression of materialization. The sacraments are said to be means by which grace comes to men. In this way grace is conceived of as an almost material thing, certainly as something that can be separated from God, something self-subsistent that is given to men through a ritual. On these terms, it is supposed, grace is not

conceived of as a personal fellowship with God, but as something objective and material. It is true that all too often the idea of the sacraments as means of grace is thought of in a far too materialistic, mechanical way by large sections of the faithful. Notions such as "piling up" grace, or "collecting" graces, or "treasury of grace", and "grace-capital" are proofs of this. And does not even our interpretation of the liturgy as a means of life point in the same direction?

3. The danger of materialization is seen finally in the various ceremonies, gestures, prayer-formulae, all of which are prescribed in detail. None is permitted to make up his own prayers. It is laid down that only set prayers be used. In this way how can there be any real expression of something personal? Not only the gifts from on high, but also the gifts men offer to God consist in an external, material relationship, it is said. The notion, widespread amongst the faithful, that participation in the liturgy is predominantly a service rendered and an activity, has its roots – so it is thought – in the nature of the Christian liturgy itself. Even prayer is no expression of the devotion of a human *I* to the divine *Thou*, but the discharge of a work of duty. But there is more. The liturgical acts, it is said, are full of material things. The liturgy uses water, wine, oil, bread, salt, etc. The use of these material things is strictly regulated. What has all this to do with a personal meeting, with the free turning of man to God?

The objections brought forward all say in effect – to put it briefly – that man's direct personal approach to God is endangered or even prevented by the liturgy.

Personal realization through the liturgy

Fundamental thinking is required in dealing with the questions which have been posed.

Religion is man's relationship towards God. Because the true depth and centre of man is his being a person, religion is man's personal relationship to God. This order has been destroyed by sin so that in his own strength man can no longer achieve a full and untroubled meeting with God. How does Christ affect this situation which exists between man and God? In Christ, man's longing for a meeting and fellowship with God is fulfilled. Through Christ God speaks to men. This he does in a manner and with a fulness hitherto unknown. The *Son* of the Father, the eternal *Word* of God becomes united with a man, thus effecting a meeting between God and man that transcends all human longing, that is incomprehensible, unsurpassable, unique. It is the word of love that God announces in his incarnate *Word*. Nothing proves the desire of God for a meeting with man so much as the fact that God became man. And because Christ is at the same time true man, he also makes man's response to the Word of God. Christ's relation to the Father is one of perfect love and total self-giving; thus it represents perfect fellowship between God and man. And so in the incarnate Son of God the personal relationship between God and man is perfected in unsurpassable measure. Those who believe in Christ gain a share in this fellowship between God and man which Christ has realized. Faith as personal surrender binds a man so closely with Christ that he shares in Christ's fellowship with the Father. Within this reality of faith, God comes to man with his word of love, and man makes the response of love. *Through* and *in* Christ who is the *way* (John 14:6) and the *door* (John 10:9), meeting between man and God is possible. Thus, Christ is no obstacle in the way of an immediate relationship between man and God. On the contrary, he is the way along which a man reaches personal closeness to God. Through Christ a man becomes a friend, a son of God. Friendship and sonship, however, are the highest forms of personal relationship.

Now, Christ is the sacrament behind all sacraments, the unity of divine and human, of the invisible and the visible, of spirit and matter. From this we can draw conclusions affecting the questions before us. Perfect meeting between God and man does not result from a purely spiritual process, but occurs in the flesh, in the corporal, earthly existence of man. And Christ's activity in the liturgy follows the same pattern. The new mode of operation of the Lord since the descent of the Holy Spirit is nothing other than the extension of the incarnation of God in time and space. In every age men are to be led to meet God in this spiritual-material way. The fact that Christ works through the liturgy means that the liturgy can

be a way along which man attains to personal encounter with God. If we look at the real mystery of
the liturgy, at its central, invisible act, we may say
that there the meeting between God and man is
realized.

This central mystery makes it clear that the liturgy
and personal life do not stand opposed, but nourish
one another. In the liturgy a meeting between God
and man can and ought to take place. In its essence,
therefore, the liturgy provides for the fulfilment of
man's structure as a person. God meets man wherever
and whenever he will. But he has willed that man
should meet him chiefly – although not exclusively –
in the public worship of the Church. God has not lost
his freedom by this alliance. He is still perfectly free
even if he appoints the way by which man shall
come to him. Nor is man's free personal decision
abolished thereby. Quite the opposite: by his action
in the mysteries of the Church, God faces man with a
decision. True personal approach to God by man
means obediently seeking God where he allows himself to be found.

The grace mediated through the sacraments must
likewise be seen under the personal category. Grace is
not something which can be separated from God its
source and giver. Admittedly it is not simply God's
loving intention towards man, but a reality created
in us by God. But this work of God in us is the gift of
the God who loves man. In this gift God's love comes
to man, "because the charity of God is poured forth
in our hearts, by the Holy Ghost who is given to us"

(Rom. 5:5). The new life which in his love God manifests in the believer is nothing else but the new community of life with God, which is the most intense personal life. As a result, the gift given through the liturgy as well, bears a personal stamp. Grace is never a substance that can be separated from God.

The third objection starts off with the fact that the liturgy is composed of many material things and many prescribed ceremonies and rites. This seems to make personal approach to God difficult or even impossible. There is no doubt that in practice many great strains arise because of this, many dangers, misunderstandings, and even abuses. But an abuse in practice is no ground for the denial of the original and true meaning of a thing.

The numerous material objects and the many corporal actions express the fact that God desires to meet man in the reality of his earthly existence. This earthly existence of man is not purely spiritual. It is always, in every phase of his life and in every situation, at once spiritual and material. Man cannot realize his personal nature apart from his senses. Personal encounters between men, human friendship, cannot be realized purely spiritually. The bodily and physical is an expression and a bridge in personal life. The liturgy must be regarded in the same light. According to the original design, what is external and material in it is the expression of, and a help towards, personal fulfilment. Folding the hands is no obstacle in the way of true prayer – a pre-eminently personal act. The inner process is expressed in the folding or outstretching of the hands. These gestures, on the other hand, exert their influence on the spirit, and make it easier to speak to the unseen God. The same sort of thing is true when we eat the sacred bread of the Eucharist. The bread is a sign of the invisible personal gift that is received, a sign of Christ who called himself "the bread of life" (John 6:35). At the same time it also helps man to make a spiritual oblation to God.

With regard to prescribed texts it is appropriate once again to realize their original purpose. They are, first of all, the expression of a community dialogue with God, and such a dialogue has to be formal and prescribed; and then they support the individual in disciplined, orderly speech with God, free from all subjective restriction. Even in this there is no ultimate antithesis between fixed form and personal action. Here, too, there is a fundamental unity, a genuine relationship of fulfilment and help. The difficulties and dangers lie in the particular case.

One question remains to be answered: is participation in the liturgy only the performance of an act that has nothing to do with personal behaviour? Are the liturgy as human service rendered, and liturgy as personal human fulfilment antithetical?

For the members of the Church, taking part in the liturgy, is in part a duty, a command which they must obey. The believer who attends Mass on Sunday thereby fulfils a command of the Church, he performs a duty. If attendance at worship is seen exclusively as the performance of a duty, as a work which man presents to God, that certainly does not accord with the spirit of the liturgy. Intelligent participation demands a self-oblation to God of the man himself. But there exists no necessary antithesis in the liturgy, between personal oblation and the performance of a work. The purpose of the command is to lead man through external participation to a personal encounter. The one does not necessarily exclude the other. However, the temptation always threatens, that people will be content with the external discharge of what is commanded, while resisting the claim upon their complete personal turning to God. It is easier to present an outward service than to offer oneself. But the former is only of value if it is the expression of the self-oblation of the man to God.

The preconditions of personal participation in the liturgy

A personal attitude cannot be forced. It comes to be only when one man opens out towards another freely. That an encounter with God in particular cannot be forced is a fact of great moment for religious education in general. Liturgical education is· no exception. On the contrary, it must apply this fact with special care; for it is in this sphere that the temptation is acute to be content with a compulsory attendance at public worship. One can compel children to go to Mass. To make attendance at Mass become a real meeting with God is beyond the power of every pedagogic or pastoral sanction.

Conditions can and must be created, which make possible and encourage participation in worship as a personal meeting with God. Let us distinguish two kinds of such preconditions: the understanding of the actions, and the tangible form of the actions.

1. *Understanding*

Personal participation in the liturgical actions and texts is only possible if these are understood. At least a minimum of understanding is required. This means that the ceremonies and texts have to be explained. No one can share spritually in that majestic early Christian hymn, the Gloria in Excelsis of the Mass, if he does not understand it. Again: how can a person share in offering the sacrifice of the Mass if he does not know what a sacrifice is, what Christ's sacrifice is, and that the Mass is the sacramental making present of this sacrifice so that man may gain a share in it through faithful self-oblation?

It is not sufficient, however, to explain the liturgical formulae and ceremonies. The explanation must point the reason for things. Nor is it sufficient to talk very interestingly or deeply of the ceremonies at Baptism. What a long story one could make of all that! How prone one is to parade one's knowledge of liturgical history. There is nothing wrong with telling something of the history of a prayer or of a ceremony. But this must not be done merely for the sake of extending information. In liturgical education we must always keep the real end in view: that the audience are drawn into personal participation. Any instruction which neglects this is not fulfilling its function. It may be very effective, very popular, very rhetorical; but if the audience are not brought by it to a state in which they can set about the liturgical action or prayer in question as a personal activity, the whole effort has missed its real point.

The sacramentals provide a particularly rewarding subject for such instruction. In dispensing them we very often are content with the mere action and neglect any explanation of the significance. Consequently, ignorance and the danger of misunderstanding are very great in this sphere. How easy it is for people to be interested only in gaining material help! And yet all these consecrations and blessings are religious acts. The blessing of St. Blaise, for example, as the text of the prayer at the blessing of the candles and of the people clearly shows, consists in a turning to God by the minister, and his beseeching God to deliver the recipient from diseases of the throat and all other evils, through the intercession and merits of St. Blaise, "so that he may give thanks to God and praise his holy name". Thus the blessing is no magical incantation, but a true prayer through which man turns to God with a worldly request which is yet subordinated to the glory of God.

If one explains the meaning of the blessing from the text at hand, and not from some arbitrary interpretation, and if one links with it an explanation of the lighted candle and the Sign of the Cross which the ministrant makes over the recipient as a gesture of blessing, then an action in the recipient, corresponding to the objective ceremony, can result. The most propitious time for such instruction is immediately before the blessing is given. If it is done in the form of a short address, then the preacher can count on a grateful audience who will be more attentive than they are during a normal sermon. Added to the factor of novelty, which arouses a certain tension, there is a stimulus in the fact that they are learning something which they can immediately translate into action.

A well-known example of the serious way in which the blessings of the Church can be misunderstood is the Churching of Women after child-birth. Even the common term "Purification" betrays the direction in which the false interpretation, partly Old Testament, partly Manichaean, is to be sought. Here again the text of the prayers at the blessing gives us unequivocal information. According to these, this blessing of the mother is no ritual of purification, but a thanksgiving for safe delivery and a petition for God's blessing on the mother and the child. As in all blessings, here too the essential action is prayer – man speaking with God. The mother is supposed to come for this blessing with a glad heart and loving solicitude for her child, in order to offer thanksgiving and petition to God with the priest. The object of her coming is thus to meet with God. Obviously, she is capable of this personal act only if she knows the meaning of

the blessing and can join in the prayers. This cannot
be done without understanding; and understanding
presupposes instruction.

What we have shown concerning these two blessings applies to all the sacramentals and throughout
the whole extent of the Church's worship. Liturgical
instruction must bring the faithful to a point where
they recognize the liturgical celebrations as meaningful ceremonies that are to be carried out in a
personal way.

2. *The tangible form*

The second precondition of a personal performance
of worship is that the liturgical acts be well arranged.
However good instruction may be, it is not enough
to achieve the desired end. The form of the separate
acts must be such that they are not only no hindrance
to, but a positive facilitation of, intelligent action by
minister and faithful. A hurriedly said prayer is an
obstacle in the way of conscious, recollected conver-
sation with God. It cannot possibly be *recollected* in
the original sense of the word, for one is quite unable
to call to mind what the words of the prayer mean.
Hurried and hasty speech is death to personal prayer.
This applies equally to recited prayers and to corporate prayer. If corporate, public prayer is to be a
true speaking to God – and when is it not that? – it
must be a calm and worthy utterance. By this is
meant neither a slovenly, drowsy nor an emotional,
declamatory manner of speech. A simple, calm
manner of speaking helps both the faithful and the

liturgical minister to make their own the prescribed and set texts of the prayers, so that the externalized prayer of the liturgy can become a genuine expression of the devotion of each one.

Besides this, the priest or reader should speak so distinctly that he can be followed by the faithful without strain. The mother who comes to church after the birth of her child to receive the blessing, cannot thank God and entreat him in the words of this blessing if the priest speaks the prayers and the psalm in such a way that she is unable to understand them. In saying prayers the priest or reader should develop the tendency to think not of himself, but of those present, so that they can hear him easily, and, led by his words, be able truly to lift their hearts up to God. So it must be with all prayers intended for the participation of all the faithful – whether vocally or in silence. This does not apply to every prayer of the liturgy, for some of these are prayers for the liturgical minister alone, and are therefore spoken by him in a low voice. Most of the prayers and hymns of all the sacraments and sacramentals are indeed meant to be joined in by the congregation, vocally or at least mentally.

The problem of the correct form of prayer is obviously only one of many questions emerging from the demand for an intelligible form of worship. But it is a problem of special importance, because of its nature prayer represents a personal encounter of man with God. What has been said of the form of the words applies with appropriate modification to the form of every liturgical action: they all must promote personal participation.

Catechesis in the service of personal realization

The new German Catechism is a valuable aid to education in personal action. In many places we can observe the effort to make plain the personal features of a truth, and to arouse the personal powers in man. This is specially marked in the liturgical instruction. The danger for personal thinking, inherent in the stressing of the idea of community, cannot be laid to the charge of this catechism. This element is not allowed to obscure the importance of the personal element in worship. On the contrary, it is striking how much attention is paid to it.

The decisive thing for the personal understanding of worship is its Christocentric structure. Through the teaching that Christ is the principal minister in all of the sacraments, on receiving these sacraments men see themselves confronted, not by a material reality, but by a personal reality. In this reality the human *I* meets the divine *Thou*.

The personal character is also apparent in the effort to elucidate the symbolic meaning of the liturgical acts. On the other hand it should also be pointed out that this effort does not appear just here and there, but in the whole teaching of the sacraments. This is instruction which seeks to produce intelligent collaboration. We quote the explanation of the collect for the day in the Mass as a typical example. "The priest extends his hands and greets us with the words: 'Dominus vobiscum' (the Lord be with you); and we answer: 'Et cum spiritu tuo' (and with thy spirit). Then the priest invites us to pray with the word 'Oremus' (Let us pray); thereupon he extends his hands and takes up our prayer into the collect for the day. We answer with 'Amen' (so be it)." We note how this explanation shows the exchange of greetings between priest and congregation in its dialogue character, and the collect as the prayer of all. As already noted, this explanation is not peculiar, but typical. Not only the celebration of the Mass, but the dispensing of all the sacraments is explained with a view to comprehending, personal action. The high points of such instruction are to be found – apart from the explanation of the Mass – in sections 83-5 on the sacrament of Penance, and in sections 70-2 on prayer.

X

CORPORAL WORSHIP

L ITURGICAL activity is never purely spiritual;
always and everywhere it is a physical activity.
Man's body is so much an essential component
of liturgical activity that the latter is quite impossible without it. When one begins to reflect on the
objects and laws of liturgical education, unavoidably
one is forced to consider the body and its activities.
If, then, we look at the concrete, corporeal action of
man in the liturgy, at his posture and gestures for
example, and ask about its meaning, we come in the
end to the fundamental question about the nature
and purpose of man's body in general. It would
appear that the liturgy presupposes a specific
understanding of man and his body, and that, on the
other hand, there are notions about the human body
– popular, philosophical, and theological – which are
incompatible with the liturgy. We cannot, therefore,
avoid stating, at least in broad outline, the understanding of the nature of the body which the liturgy
presupposes, and which is expressed in the liturgy.
At this point we do not have to provide a systematic
basis of a philosophic or theological kind. For our
purpose it will suffice to sum up a few truths about
man and his body that are significant for our
discussion.

Faith's understanding of the body

Man's earthly existence is never anything other than corporeal. For him, separation from the body means the end of earthly life. Hence, for man, the body is not something on the fringe of reality. It is, in fact, so much tied up with the essence of earthly, human life that without it life is simply impossible. Man's purely spiritual existence after death does not contradict this truth; for, if man exists after death and before his resurrection as a personal being, he enjoys perfection of being only after his resurrection.

Man is made up of soul and body. The soul is, indeed, the higher in rank. According to the teaching of the Church it is the *forma corporis*, the formative principle of the body. But this qualitative distinction does not imply any depreciation of the body. Contradicting the truth that man is soul and body is, on one side, the idealist view which sees the spirit as everything and the body as almost nothing, a responsibility, an irksome burden, or even a prison from which the spirit must be freed. Such a view likes to assume a religious disguise. But it contradicts the Christian faith. It is a perfectly natural result for the faithful, who fall under the influence of such an anti-corporeal way of thinking, to be unable to find any living relationship with the worship of the Church.

On the other extreme we find the materialist view which denies the autonomy and distinctiveness of the spirit, and reduces all that is spiritual in man to a sublimated expression of the corporeal. It would be superfluous to explain that such a view makes, not only worship, but any kind of religion at all, impossible.

The soul and the body of man are not two entities existing side by side. Their relationship is that of organic unity, not of mechanical proximity. This unity is expressed, from the one side at least, by the formula already quoted: *anima forma corporis*. The spiritual soul is the deepest formal principle of the body. It *animates* the body and gives it its form. Man is an embodied spirit, an animated body. Thus the body is not just a tool which the soul uses. Above all it is the mode in which a man lives, the form and expression of his life in this world. Man acts thus, always in a physical way. His action in this world towards his fellow men, even his action towards God, is not of a purely spiritual sort. It is always partly determined by the body. Corporeality in religious life is specially evident in liturgical worship. Corporeal, liturgical activity is, therefore, nothing unusual, an exception to the normal life of man. It is predetermined by the fact that man is a living, organic unity of soul and body.

The body was created by God and therefore is good. This truth of faith is apparently contradicted by experience. We can *see* that the body is not good. Moreover, we see how the body with its appetites and passions has a destructive effect upon the spirit. The experiences that men have acquired in this respect during their long history no doubt account for the depreciation, the contempt of, and even hostility towards the body, as manifested in many philosophical and religious movements. Against all serious contempt of the body the Church has always defended the truth that the body was created by God and is therefore good. It is true that the order of the body has been disturbed, often destroyed, by sin. The disorderly desires of the sensual faculties – in themselves a masterpiece of the Creator – and sickness and death are consequences of original sin. The dreadful disfigurement of the body through undisciplined appetites, sickness and death – all that is taken very seriously by the Christian faith. The affirmation of faith that the body was created by God and therefore fundamentally good, is not based on a naïve interpretation of life. Faith sees the body as realistically as unbelief. But it looks deeper and sees through disorder to the divine origin. Were the human body nothing but a contemptible and wicked instrument – after the fashion of Gnostic or Manichaean philosophy – to which the soul is tied as a kind of punishment, then it would have no function within liturgical celebration. In that case the corporeal action in religious life would have to be reduced to the very minimum. A liturgy expressed in visible forms would then be impossible. But the Christian faith teaches that because the whole man was created by God, the body, too, is to give glory to God.

What the Christian faith says about the body as a creation of God testifies to its dignity and worth.

Not until the Incarnation, however, did God reveal completely how much he still valued the body as his handiwork, and how incomprehensibly great his plans are for re-shaping it anew for eternal glory. All the great events and actions in the life of Christ took place in the bodily sphere: birth, passion, death, resurrection, and ascension. John the evangelist describes the Incarnation quite simply as a *becoming flesh*. "The Word was made flesh" (John 1:14), he says in an almost offensive way against any Docetic watering down that would suggest that Christ had not had a real body. The whole earthly life of Christ was a true human life, hence a real bodily life. This corporeality of the incarnate Logos reached its climax in death as the sacrifice of his body, in the Resurrection as the beginning of a new glorified corporeality, and in the Ascension as the ultimate sharing of this body in the divine majesty.

The body in the liturgy

That God comes to men in a bodily way in the worship of the Church as well, is founded upon the fact of the incarnation of the divine Word. In the liturgy God advances further along the way which he had begun in the Incarnation. There, he desires to meet men, not in a purely spiritual way, from soul to soul, but corporeally, through bodily actions and material things. It is in line with this if God desires man, from his side, to approach him in a like manner, in the totality of his being, in body and soul.

The way of corporeality which God chooses to follow has a multiple goal: he means, first, to make the invisible visible – bread and wine indicate the hidden divine food; then, he means to impart the divine gifts – after the Consecration, bread and wine actually become this food; and finally, it is the foundation for the eternal transfiguration of the human body and of the whole world.

The last point is worthy of special note because it is not always seen and prized enough, although it is of decisive importance for the relationship between the liturgy and the human body. The *eternal salvation* which God gives man through Christ does not consist only of salvation for the soul, but of salvation for the whole man, soul and body. Man in his completeness is called to salvation; and the sayings about *eternal life* must likewise be understood in the same way. This eternal life embraces the body also. In its own appropriate way, the body shares in divine transfiguration. God offers this salvation, this life, to men through the sacraments. And so, through them God aims at not merely the sanctification of the soul, but also the renewal and sanctification of the body. This is not to assert that the body will be changed in its physical condition. But it does mean that the sacraments are laying the foundations of future transfiguration.

The second goal, too, requires some clarification. Like many material things, the body is an instrument of grace. Grace comes to man by way of the senses.

This applies not only to the grace that man receives through the sacraments, but even to those graces that man receives apart from the sacraments, by faith. For faith comes by hearing, and hearing from preaching (Rom. 10:14-17). Now, speaking and hearing are functions of the senses, activities of the body; and so, even in the spiritual act of faith man's body is active. The action of the body as a mediator of grace reaches its height, however, in the celebration of the liturgy. Here again we must first of all remember the part played by the word. There is always speech when any sacrament is dispensed. Without words there can be no sacrament. At Baptism the baptismal formula, "I baptize thee in the name of the Father, and of the Son, and of the Holy Spirit," must be spoken. Bread and wine are not consecrated unless the words of institution are read. In short without the bodily activity of speaking there can be no sacramental act.

The activity of the body comes even more clearly into view if we think of the use of material things in worship. For example, at Baptism grace is given only when the water actually touches the body of the baptized. A mere symbolic pouring of water would not effect grace. Again, at Confirmation the forehead of the confirmed is anointed with holy oil. On the part of the minister and of the recipient this anointing is a bodily act. The most concrete expression of this circumstance is found in the Eucharistic meal, when only those receive the Lord's body who eat the bread. All of these examples illustrate the fact that sacramental grace can only be mediated through material things if these are brought into contact with the body of the recipient. In other words: the grace of the sacraments is only imparted to the human soul through the mediation of the body.

Bodily posture and gestures

Not only the mediation of grace, but also the turning of man to God in the liturgy proceeds along bodily lines. There is no action in public worship which does not involve the body. This is true of the simplest gestures, as of the most solemn celebrations. Man always acts through his body. He speaks, listens, sees, sings, stands, and kneels. These various forms of bodily activity are not just utilitarian in purpose. Their symbolism is even more important. An appreciation of them is a condition of a properly ordered activity. In what follows let us explain the symbolism of some of these postures and gestures.

1. Standing

A posture, adopted almost all the time by the liturgical minister, and frequently, by the faithful, is the posture of standing. What does this symbolize at worship? Obviously, standing has a purely utilitarian purpose as well. Often the priest is obliged to stand to perform some action. We need only think of the presentation of the sacrifice and the distribution of the consecrated bread. But standing has a purpose over and above that of mere utility. That is to say, it is also an expression of an inner spiritual process. What idea, then, is expressed in the posture of standing?

Standing expresses primarily the redemption, the fundamental reality of Christian existence. By standing erect the believer affirms that he is no longer a bound slave, but a redeemed and free man, a son or daughter of God, one who has risen to eternal life with God. In the early Church for a time it was forbidden to pray kneeling during the season of Easter. In those days Christians took the standing position very seriously as a witness to belief in the Resurrection. Even today the liturgy still knows of this standing of the redeemed sons and daughters of the heavenly Father. When in the Eucharist we *make bold* to say the Our Father, we rise. Likewise we stand to say the Gloria and the Preface and Sanctus, those great hymns of thanksgiving for redemption.

Standing can also embody the idea of reverence. Hence the congregation rise to hear the Gospel, to show reverence to the words of our Lord. Another idea is close to reverence: readiness. When one is standing reverently before a superior, this erect posture can be a sign of readiness to do his bidding. Thus it is with the standing for the Gospel. Besides reverence this is supposed to indicate readiness to carry out the wishes of our Lord who is speaking to us in the Gospel. This idea of readiness is also expressed by standing for the creed. In the creed the believer professes his readiness to accept the Word of God which he hears, in all its fulness, and to confess it publicly, that is to defend it if need be.

If these ideas are to be expressed through the posture of standing, then a condition must be fulfilled. It is not just any standing that embodies the idea. A slovenly standing position does not embody joy at redemption nor pride in the new dignity of the Christian. Standing in which one goes all to pieces spoils reverence and shows no readiness. Only an upright, alert and recollected standing position is a suitable expression for the ideas mentioned.

Because the priest stands throughout the whole celebration of the Eucharist and is seen by the people, he is specially bound to feel a constant responsibility in this. But the congregation, too, must be taught to stand not at the gospel only. They should stand at least for the great prayers as well, for the Preface and the Our Father. As well as this they should be taught – particularly the youth – to understand and affirm the meaning of this standing, and make an effort to stand properly.

2. Kneeling

Kneeling is a totally different posture from standing. One might almost say that it is the very opposite. Kneeling, a man makes himself small. He does not want to announce his greatness, but his abasement. In the true sense, man need kneel only to God. In this way he acknowledges God as the Lord of his life, as the supremely great and infinitely powerful

One, and at the same time as the creator who has called him out of nothing. Kneeling can even go to the length of complete prostration upon the ground. This form occurs in the liturgy at the beginning of the Good Friday service and at ordination. Kneeling is the attitude of adoration, the recognition of God as God.

In kneeling, however, a man wants to express something else as well. Man is not only a creature: he is also a sinner in the eyes of God. Sin lies upon him like a burden that forces him to the ground. Even more strongly than that it arouses the sense that one cannot exist before God. And so one kneels to confess one's sins in the sacrament of Penance, and at the Confiteor of Mass and Compline. The priest, it is true, does not kneel at the Confiteor, but makes a deep bow as a sign of his sinfulness. This bowing of head and trunk expresses the same sort of thing as does kneeling: humility, adoration, and confession of guilt.

Kneeling and bowing down do not rob a man of his dignity. They express our true relationship to God. To admit this truth is never unworthy of us; on the contrary, such admission is always full of dignity. The kneeling of a Christian is not the kneeling of a slave, but of a son who is both creature and sinner. It is always a confession of God as creator and as holy. Kneeling and bowing down express man's humility, which is nothing but the recognition and affirmation of our creaturely existence.

Again, of this bodily attitude it must also be said

that not every kneeling is an expression of humility and a proof of adoration. Kneeling also – very specially – should be performed well and correctly, not carelessly and comfortably. It requires conscious discipline.

Liturgical education will also have to touch on genuflexion. What goes by this name is very often nothing better than a timid apology for this bodily posture. A non-Catholic would find it very difficult to deduce from such a truncated gesture that the believer wanted to make thereby an act of adoration.

3. *Gestures of the hands*

Human hands are powerfully expressive. They are not just useful tools, but channels through which his soul may express itself. In the liturgy they make possible a whole series of significant gestures, that fulfil predominantly a non-utilitarian, a symbolic function. Thus the confession of sins is underlined by the striking of the breast. The extending of the hands over the people indicates the imparting of grace. The Sign of the Cross which people make upon themselves or upon others is a gesture of blessing. But chiefly it is prayers that are accompanied by gestures of the hands.

Even today the liturgical minister has to say or sing the chief prayers of the Mass in the so-called *orante* posture. In this the hands are raised and held apart. In earlier times the faithful, too, prayed in this attitude. Ancient Christian art knew the picture of the *orante* as an image of the Church at prayer.

The Church is, indeed, the society of the redeemed who turn to God and open themselves to him in prayer. The *orante* posture is a prayer-attitude that was well-known everywhere in antiquity, and that is explicity mentioned in the Scriptures. St. Paul, the apostle, commands it even when writing to the young Timothy: "I will therefore that men pray in every place, lifting up pure hands" (I Tim. 2:8). It is remarkable that this attitude of prayer, in spite of explicit apostolic prescription, could have become so much neglected by Christians. And yet, how wonderfully suited it is to Christian prayer! An upright and open posture, having about it something liberated and free, is most becoming in the redeemed. It declares that the heart is being raised up to God, that one is turning to God "above" in praise, thanksgiving, and supplication, and finally that one is open to receive divine grace.

As we have said, today the liturgy still knows this beautiful and significant gesture when it prescribes it for the priest saying the principal prayers at the Eucharist. It is specially meaningful at the Eucharistic Prayer where it represents the response to the invitation with which the prayer begins: "Lift up your hearts."

The liturgy does not know of prayer with clasped hands, but it does allow for prayer with hands folded together. This seems to have a Teutonic origin and has crept into the liturgy since the early Middle Ages. When a vassal took an oath to his feudal superior he placed his closed hands within those of his feudal superior. In this way he acknowledged him as his lord and signified his subjection to him. The liturgy still retains this ceremony in the ordination of a priest, when the newly-ordained lays his folded hands within those of the bishop. At prayer the folded hands signify a submission to God, the surrender to God as Lord of life, and so adoration of God. It also expresses supplication.

4. *The Sign of the Cross*

One of the most meaningful and frequently used gestures of the hands is the Sign of the Cross. It is the gesture with which the Catholic Christian is accustomed to accompany his daily prayers, and which is used by the liturgical minister in every sacrament and sacramental. Because used so frequently it runs the risk of becoming too familiar. Often enough people have only a vague notion of its meaning, and the way it is made is not always dignified or correct.

There are various forms of the Sign of the Cross. The priest makes it as a sign of blessing upon the faithful, upon animals, and things; it is known as the little Sign of the Cross upon the forehead, the lips, and breast; finally it can be made as a large Sign of the Cross upon oneself. This is the commonest form.

When making the Sign of the Cross, one raises the right hand to the forehead, then moves it to the breast, and then finally from the left to the right shoulder. The movement of the hand is accompanied by the words: "In the name of the Father, and of the

Son, and of the Holy Ghost." What is the meaning behind this gesture? Why do we place the hand on the forehead when we name the Father, upon the breast when we name the Son, and move it from the left to the right shoulder when we invoke the Holy Spirit? Let us explain the significance from a biblical incident.

After Jesus' Baptism in the Jordan there occurred a unique theophany. The gospel of St. Matthew reports: "And Jesus being baptized, forthwith came out of the water; and lo, the heavens were opened to him, and he saw the Spirit of God descending as a dove and coming upon him. And, behold, a voice from heaven saying: This is my beloved Son, in whom I am well pleased" (Matt. 3:16 f.). This is the one and only time in the whole history of revelation that God has announced himself as a Trinity of Persons. This revelation characterizes each of the three divine Persons. The Father remains hidden on high. He is the invisible origin and beginning. Only his Word can be heard. The Son, on the other hand, can be seen. He stands upon the earth in human form. By his incarnation the Son is God made visible upon this earth. In him God has stepped down from the heights, that is, out of his supra-mundane secrecy, and become visible. The Holy Spirit hovers between the Father and the Son in the form of a dove, the personal unity and fellowship of Father and Son. Thus the mystery of God's inner life is unveiled.

In the Sign of the Cross we witness to and confess this revelation of God. By laying our hand upon our forehead we bear witness to the Father, the invisible origin of all things. Laying the hand upon the breast we confess the incarnation of God in Jesus Christ. And when the hand moves from one shoulder to the other this points to the Holy Spirit who is called the bond between Father and Son. How vividly this movement of the hand expresses this peculiar property of the Spirit! And so the Sign of the Cross reflects the theophany of the Trinity: the Father sends the Son in the Holy Spirit.

The revelation of God at the Jordan discloses a second mystery. It reveals the love in God, and the love of God for man. The Father utters the word of love: "This is my beloved Son." The Spirit is depicted as the Spirit of love, for the dove is a symbol of love. And the human form of the Son of God is the form of the love of God coming down to men. Let us observe the two stages in this revelation of God's love. The Father reveals his love through the word. Then the Spirit makes it more vivid in the form of an animal. Here we not only hear a voice speaking, but we see love depicted. The love of God is made completely visible in the incarnate One. For, that God has become visible in a man, is the perfection of God's self-revelation. In this we have a second meaning for the Sign of the Cross. When a Christian makes the Sign of the Cross he declares God to be the God of love.

Finally we must speak of a significance attached to the Sign of the Cross that, from outward appearance, is the most obvious. This only acquires its full depth, however, when linked with the above mentioned meanings. Never and nowhere has the love of God for man been more powerfully and tangibly declared than in the death of the incarnate Son of God upon the Cross. We bear witness to this event by the Sign of the Cross. On the Cross God broke the power of the Devil and brought about the redemption of the world. The Cross is thus the sign of God's sovereignty and of the world's redemption. It is more full of meaning than is any other sign: it is, quite simply, the sign of the Christian faith.

XI

THE ARRANGEMENT OF THE PLACE OF WORSHIP

THE formal arrangement of the celebration of public worship is the central problem for liturgical education. Everything in the liturgy, in the celebration of the sacraments, the sacramentals, the Divine Office, cries out for tangible expression. Everything should find a genuine and worthy form. All that goes to make up man's bodily action must be appropriately formed. The corporate ceremonies in public worship, too, must be moulded along the same lines. We say "corporate ceremonies" advisedly. If the form of the Mass represents the most important problem, nonetheless, it is not the only one. The celebration of every sacrament, the dispensing of every sacramental, and the performance of every part of the Divine Office ought to be ruled by the immutable law which demands an appropriate external form. The problem of suitable formation, however, points to yet a third sphere. The place where public worship takes place must also be arranged in the right way. As a rule, this place is a church, a house of God. Most of the sacraments are celebrated within it. First and foremost, the church is there for the celebration of the liturgy. True, it is also used for extra-liturgical activities, principally for devotions and private prayers. But it is primarily the place where the liturgy is celebrated. The extent to which the liturgy can be properly and suitably celebrated depends also upon the arrangement of the place of worship. From the many problems which arise in this field, let us select a few of special importance. We shall deal with the setting out of the nave, the altar, the pulpit, and the baptistry. These problems can be approached from various angles. We shall deal with them from the point of view of liturgical education. Hence we exclude aesthetic and rubrical problems.[1]

The house of God

In heathen religions the temple was regarded as the house of the god because his image stood there. It was thought that the god's presence was attached to this image. The Christian faith, however, knows that "God dwelleth not in temples made with hands" (Acts 17:24). But there is a place upon this earth where the real presence of the one, true, living God resides. This place consists of those men who have taken God into themselves through faith in the Son of God, who has appeared in human form. In a real sense they are "habitations of God" (Eph. 2:22) and "houses of God" (I Tim. 3:15). Christian believers individually and all together, that is as the Church,

[1] Cf. *Const.*, art. 122f, esp. 124 and 128. The *Constitution* is concerned, unlike the author, with aesthetic problems, and only broaches the question of liturgical education in this context in the most general terms.

are the "house of God". Thus the apostle St. Paul can write: "For you are the temple of the living God" (II Cor. 6:16). This thought is perfectly in line with the preaching of Jesus. Christ promised to any who loves him that, "We will come to him and make our abode with him" (John 14:23). This dwelling in the man who believes is so concrete, so corporeal, that the body itself is described as a house of God: "Know you not that your members are the temple of the Holy Ghost, who is in you. . . ?" (I Cor. 6:19).

The living house of God, made up of people of flesh and blood, requires as a rule, although not always, a place of worship where they can hear the Word of God, receive his graces, and together offer him thanksgiving, praise, and supplication. This is the house of God in stone and lime. The *living* Church needs a church built of stone or brick or wood. This will be there for the celebration of the public worship of the people of God. For the sake of its dignity and sanctity it receives a special dedication.

The Eucharist is the centre of the public worship of the Church. The prime function of a church is to make its regular celebration possible. The liturgical value of a church must be measured primarily, therefore, by the way in which it fulfils this function. Modern church architecture everywhere is showing a real effort to be true to this function. A church has, however, other functions. It is there also for the administering of the other sacraments, for the adoration of the Blessed Sacrament, for devotions, and for private prayer. The dignity and beauty of churches is often extolled, and rightly. Nonetheless, the fact must not be overlooked that they are not everlasting and imperishable. As constantly threatened artifacts they are an appropriate symbol of the living Church; for this does not yet enjoy assured and final possession of the divine presence. Like their Old Testament forefathers, the people of God are still pilgrims and, like them too, still live in tents. That the Church is the tabernacle, that is the *tent* of God, is characteristic of the essence of both the spiritual and the stone house of God. Only when the day of the new creation dawns will all that is temporary, transient, and imperfect be over and done with. Then the people of God will no longer require any special place of worship. Then the whole world will be the place of the manifest presence of divine majesty, in the true and complete sense, "the city of God" (cf. Apoc. 21).

The nave of the church

The art of church building today has taken up the problems of the liturgical arrangement of the house of God as no earlier period has ever done. In the main, architects are taking great pains to build churches so that they do not make the celebration of the liturgy difficult, but easier. Their special concern is to arrange everything in the church so that it assists the corporate performance of divine worship. This is shown, for example, in the construction of the nave of the church. The liturgical revival aims at turning private worshippers into a single community celebrating public worship together. The attainment of this end is hindered if the church is built having two, three, or even more, aisles. This style of construction prevents all the congregation from seeing the altar. Moreover it weakens the congregation's sense of unity. And so today, as a rule, churches are built as the enclosure of a single space. The faithful are no longer divided up by pillars and buttresses. Such devices have been superseded in modern building techniques, but if they do happen to be used, they are set around the area occupied by the people, separating it only from the side passages. Thus the body of the church is built as a unified space enclosing everybody.

What effect does such a form of nave have? First of all it expresses the truth that all the faithful make up a society, the new people of God. This architectural form allows the faithful to be seen as a congregation assembled for corporate public worship, and not as the sum of individuals at prayer, each one intent on his own business. Over and above this, the uninterrupted, unified nave gives the faithful a sense of belonging together. They feel, without thinking about it consciously, that they are a community. This is not to say that such a feeling cannot exist in a church built in the Gothic style with several aisles. If public worship has a lively form, that feeling is perfectly possible. But in spite of this reservation, it is still true that, seen purely from the point of view of the effect of the surrounding space, a church built as a unity will more readily stimulate the sense of community.

The third advantage is that from everywhere there is an unimpeded view of the altar. This unimpeded view of the altar is now taken for granted. The eye of everyone is drawn almost irresistibly to the altar. Once again the important function of observing the liturgical actions can be realized by all of the faithful. A functionally correct building thus puts the faithful in a position to take full part in worship.

So that participation be keen, it is also a good thing if the nave tends to breadth rather than too great length. It is strange that this fact has not yet received enough attention in the church building of our time. We may mention two churches by the Swiss architect Fritz Metzger that have produced eminently successful solutions along these lines. The churches are St. Francis' in Basle and St. Regula's in Zürich. These churches are neither long nor circular buildings, but have broad naves. Anywhere in them one has the feeling of being near the altar. Such a form of nave strengthens the feeling of unity amongst the worshippers and makes vision easier. The nearer the worshippers are to the sanctuary, the better can they see the actions of the celebrant and so take part in them, and the more difficult is it for them to persevere in the role of passive onlookers. The arrangement of the nave which emphasizes the breadth rather than the length would correspond to the aim

of the liturgical revival to build churches as places
for corporate celebrations.

The altar

In his first letter to the congregation at Corinth
(I Cor. 10:21) St. Paul calls the altar "the table of
the Lord". The altar is the table of the Lord because
upon it the Lord himself prepares the royal marriage
feast for his guests. From this table he hands out to
his own people, the "bread of life", the "cup of
salvation" – himself. At the same time the altar is
the stone of sacrifice upon which the sacrifice of the
Lamb of God is made present sacramentally. If it is
made to signify Christ, this is a purely symbolic idea.
It has a further significance as the exalted place where
God is offered obeisance and honour.

Although the essential functions of the altar are
unchanging, in the course of centuries the altar has
taken very different forms. We need only think of the
Gothic altar and the Baroque altar. The modern
tendency is clearly to free the altar from all unnecessary accretions. Thus we no longer see a reredos,
or pictures or statues upon the altar. One is afraid of
attracting attention to these rather than to the table
itself, so that the altar might no longer be seen as a
table or a place of sacrifice.

Some have described this radical change in the
form of the altar as the expression of an austere,
unimaginative puritanism or of cold rationalism.
This is a misunderstanding. There is much more to it

than that. In this return to the original and the
essential, it is true that the influence of the sentiment
of modern man has been at work. But the determining forces have been in the sphere of the liturgy. For
the sake of the sublimity and dignity of the altar, this
mysterious place of the divine presence, all that is not
necessary for the celebration of the mysteries is to be
kept away. Not for the sake of a restoration, but for
the sake of the thing itself do we reach back into
early times. In his book, *Der christliche Altar* (II 542),
J. Braun, S.J., writes: "The decisive factor that
prevented the reredos from appearing for such a long
time was the ancient, deep-seated custom, not to
have anything upon the altar except the sacred
utensils – chalice, paten, the sacred books and the
pyx with the Blessed Sacrament. The reason for this
lay in the reverent awe for the holiness and dignity
of the altar. The place of the holy sacrifice, it ought
to be reserved for this sublime purpose alone, and be
used for nothing else. Even candles and the cross
were kept away from the altar. Until the eleventh
century these are regularly to be found behind the
altar."

It is aimed, then, to have a simple and unadorned
form of altar, so that the original purpose of the altar
will once again stand out unambiguously. Because
the reredos with its sometimes enormous pictures and
statues tended to overshadow the altar itself, we now
reject it altogether. The simplicity of our modern
altars must not, therefore, be misinterpreted. It is not
the sign of artistic incompetence, at least not basic-

ally or in general. It may well be that many modern altars· are not the product of great artistic ability. Architects and builders have often taken too little trouble over their altars. There is a noble simplicity of form that is of the greatest artistic merit. There is, however, a simplicity that results from a lack of creative imagination. Who would deny that some of our modern altars owe their production to this lack? This, however, is an aesthetic point, important no doubt, but not our concern at the moment. The simple form of the altar arises not primarily from aesthetic, but from liturgical motives. In it the desire is revealed to make the nature of the altar visible in an outward form. The nature of the Christian altar is to be the "table of the Lord".

The simple and unequivocal table-form of the altar also expresses the fact that what takes place there is something for the whole fellowship. A table is there for a community meal. Thus it was at the first Christian altar, at the table of the Last Supper. Christ sat at table with the twelve in order to share a meal with them. And so it must also have been in early centuries where the number of the faithful was very small. But even in apostolic times this ceased for the most part to be any longer so.

Not only the form of the altar, but its location too, is undergoing a change today. For centuries the altar had stood in the apse, immediately in front of the end wall of the choir. That is, it stood – or stands – at the very place that was furthest away from the nave of the people. This is the expression of a profound change in the conception of public worship since the early Middle Ages. The liturgy was no longer celebrated as the worship of all the faithful, but predominantly of the clergy. Hence the altar no longer had to be near the people. It was moved as far away as possible. Often now, the faithful are no longer even *onlookers*, for they cannot see what is going on at the altar; they "hear" Mass, and "assist at" it.

Because in our day the consciousness has sprung to life once more that the liturgy is the celebration of all the members of the Church, this location of the altar has begun to create problems. The remoteness of the altar makes a community celebration difficult, as we can easily see. And so the altar is brought out from the depths of the choir and placed near the congregation. According to the *Instructio de arte sacra*, published on June 30, 1952, by the Congregation of the Holy Office, the altar should be placed so that "it can be seen by all". J. Braun, S.J., already quoted, says that "the most fitting, the most beautiful, and also the most ancient way" (*Op. cit.* I 407) of placing the altar, is to place it in the open so that it can be walked around on every side. In this way too it can be completely incensed. An altar in the open also makes possible a celebration "versus populum".

If the altar is placed near the body of the church, this has the advantage that all the faithful can see and so take part better. But it also has the advantage that this position – like the form of the altar – declares that what is happening at the altar is being done for the congregation and should be done with their co-operation.

The pulpit

At the celebration of the Eucharist the Church preaches the Word of God and distributes the body of the Lord. Both are dispensed from the altar. The body of the Lord is distributed at the Communion rail. There, too, is found a place for the preaching of the Word, for the chancel-rail, the dividing mark between the sanctuary and the body of the church, used to be the place from which the Gospel was preached. Later on when churches became larger the preacher's chair – sometimes the sermon was preached from a sitting position – was moved into the nave so that the preacher would be as close as possible to the people. The shifting of the pulpit from the altar was not, indeed, a purely structural change aiming at a physical effect. It betrayed a profounder and more momentous happening: the sermon frequently became detached from the worship, not only externally, but spiritually as well. Today we are in the process of reversing these trends and incorporating the sermon within the Mass once again. All this must once again find architectural expression. In the churches of our day the ambos, pulpits at the altar-rails, are already almost taken for granted. In this way the pulpit comes close to the altar, and the connection between altar and preaching becomes apparent once again.

The pulpit is the place where the Word of God is preached. Word and sacrament come from the Lord.

The Lord feeds his people with his Word and with his body. The altar is the table from which the Lord takes up this food. It has a powerful symbolic effect if the Word of God is dispensed from the very same place as his body, from the Lord's table. If for practical reasons this food cannot be given right at the altar, then the Communion rail, where it usually is given, should be seen to be in the closest relation to the altar. At all events, the faithful must without effort realize that from around the Lord's table the Word and the body of the Lord are distributed so that *communio*, the union of Head and members, be effected.

The font

The return to the essential and the original – so characteristic of modern church architecture – reveals itself not least in the careful arrangement of the baptistry. The font is no longer pushed into some out of the way niche in the church where it remains almost unnoticed. It is placed rather in a baptistry, a special room for baptisms. This emphasis on the font corresponds to the sense of the greatness and significance of Baptism as the "bath of re-birth" to eternal life, a sense which the liturgical revival has won again for our times. The baptistry is where a man is born again to sonship of God and to a new life of fellowship with God "of water and the Holy Ghost" (John 3:5). The Johannine interpretation of Baptism is supplemented by the Pauline image of dying and rising again. In the font of Baptism the old, sinful man, doomed to death, dies, and the new man, delivered from sin and death, rises to life. Because this is a dying and a rising with Christ (Rom. 6:3-11), incorporation in Christ results. Inseparable from this incorporation in Christ, however, is incorporation as a member in the Church, his mystical body. The depth of what happens in Baptism is reflected in the wealth of ideas associated with the font. It is the place of dying, of purification, of generation. Baptism is the sacrament of beginning and initiation. It is the door through which man enters into Christ and the Church. The Roman Ritual describes Baptism as "the gate into the Christian religion and into eternal life", and asserts that the "fitting place" for the font is at the entrance to the church. The font must not be put in any old unobtrusive corner. On the other hand, the sanctuary is not a fitting place for it either. It is in accord with the nature of the first sacrament, and with the tradition of the Church, to place the font near the entrance to the church. If the font is housed in a special baptistry, this increases its importance. Modern architecture can show many beautiful examples of baptistries or even baptismal chapels.

Summing-up

By taking one or two examples, we have explained how important for the task of liturgical education arrangement of the place of worship is. It is neither immaterial nor of secondary importance, how the house of God is constructed and furnished. Not only big things, but small ones, too, demand a functional and business-like construction. The basic demand applies to everything about the place of worship and its equipment. The effect of a rationally designed house of God can be very great. Such a church may exert a profound influence upon the faithful, especially upon the children, through the channel of functional education. As a result of the rationalism, which is still working out its baneful effects in religious education, this influence is not always recognized. The one-sided stress on *ratio* is the cause of this over-estimate of the role of instruction and cognition, and the neglect of the importance of activity and of the concrete. But because the liturgy is an activity, laying claim to the whole man, liturgical education must mould the whole man, spirit and body. Such total education thus presupposes not just instruction, but also the formation of all external actions and things, of all ceremonies, and of the place and its furniture. Only under these conditions will liturgical education be able to expand and have its full effect.

XII

PREACHING AND THE
LITURGY

Redemption through word and sacrament

THE normal time for preaching is during public
worship. This is in harmony with the tradition
of the Church and, as we shall see, with the
nature of preaching itself. There are, of course, forms
of preaching outside the framework of public worship.
This, too, is in line with tradition and with the
purpose of preaching. But between preaching in
general and public worship there exists a deeper and
more essential connection.[1]

Christian preaching, wherever and whenever it
occurs, is a preaching of salvation. But the saviour is
Jesus Christ, who laid the foundation for the salvation of every individual in the whole world by his
life in Palestine, and has been applying it to each
generation ever since the first Christian feast of
Pentecost, through the Church. This contemporary
application is achieved principally through the liturgy. Because, as has been said, preaching is a
message of salvation, it is of necessity linked with the
liturgy. This does not mean that every sermon must
explicitly advert to this connection. The degree of
connection, moreover, can vary considerably. But

[1] Cf. *Const.* art. 35.

158

the decisive thing is that the connection is there, even if unexpressed. The real depth of this connection only becomes evident when we reflect that the Gospel is the "word of salvation" not merely in the sense that it proclaims this salvation, but also in the sense that by its preaching salvation already dawns. Through the word is begun that which is consummated in the sacrament.

Liturgy as preaching

When we speak of preaching we usually mean preaching through the spoken word. But there is another form of preaching. The apostle St. Paul writes, for example, the following sentence to the Church at Corinth: "For as often as you shall eat this bread and drink the chalice, you shall show the death of the Lord, until he come" (I Cor. 11:26). In this passage the apostle is not writing about preaching in words, but of a preaching by a bodily, liturgical action. Eating the bread and drinking the wine, accompanied by prayer, is an act of preaching. It proclaims the Lord's death. By celebrating Christ's meal, the assembly are confessing and proclaiming the Lord, the sacrificed and risen Lord indeed, as a present reality. Thus the liturgical celebration is not just a means of grace, but preaching as well.[2]

It is not only the Eucharist as an action that bears

[2] There is more in detail about this connection and its foundation in the Bible, in the commendable book by H. Schlier: *Die Verkündigung im Gottesdienst* (1953).

the stamp of preaching. The prayers and hymns, too, proclaim the Word of God to the faithful. This applies pre-eminently to the Eucharistic Prayer, that is the prayer that begins with the Preface and ends with the Our Father. In this solemn prayer, which used to be said or sung loudly in the early Church, the assembly proclaim, with thanksgiving and praise, the redemptive work of God in Christ. In this way the prayer becomes a form of preaching. The same sort of thing applies to the other prayers and hymns. These are primarily, it is true, prayers, that is words, addressed by the congregation to God. But because in them the faith is declared – and much of their substance comes from holy Scripture – they take on the character of preaching. Finally, there is a part of the liturgy which bears the stamp of preaching even more clearly. The celebration of the Mass and also the Divine Offices all contain lessons from holy Scripture. Most Masses contain two, many three or even more lessons. One is always a portion from one of the four gospels. The other lessons are taken from the other books of the Old and New Testaments. Every Hour of the Divine Office contains a lesson from holy Scripture. When these lessons are read out, this is not a reading of just any literary work, but the proclamation of the message of God: it is preaching.

To sum up: wherever the Church celebrates public worship, it confesses and preaches the Gospel of God. However important the sermon at Mass may be, public worship without a sermon is not necessarily worship without preaching. The liturgy is already preaching simply by its lessons, its ceremonies, its prayers and hymns. This short study has already made it clear how close and essential is the connection between the liturgy and preaching. We shall see that this goes even deeper.

The sermon as worship

If it is true that in a certain respect the liturgy is preaching, so it is true that the sermon is worship. For the sermon, in so far as it is preaching, that is, a proclamation of the Word of God, is more than the imparting of truths and commandments. Through it the coming of God and his grace is effected. God himself acts upon the hearers through the Word mediated through the preacher. The hearers, provided they are genuine hearers, receive more than just an increase in religious knowledge. By hearing in faith they accept the coming of God, his sovereignty, and his grace. In this way they are serving and honouring God. Seen in this light the sermon is "divine service" in the twofold and complete sense. This, however, is the action which lies at the heart of the liturgy. It can be described as the essence of Christian "divine service", that is public worship. It follows, then, that the sermon is worship; it is a part of the liturgy. To preach during Mass is not, therefore, to interrupt the liturgy, but on the contrary to perfect it. To think of the sermon as merely instruction is to miss its essential nature. A ministration of the Word of God, it is nothing less than a worshipful act.

The problem of form

Some practical consequences arise out of these considerations.

We have said that in their various modes, the liturgical ceremonies, prayers, hymns, and lessons all share the nature of preaching. Whether or not these various forms of worship do, in fact, say something to those present depends upon the way they are presented. The manner in which the liturgical acts are performed determines the extent and intensity of their effectiveness as preaching. It is nonsensical to state on the one hand that public worship exercises the function of preaching, while on the other hand neglecting to pay heed to the form of the actions. The truth that liturgical ceremonies declare the faith categorically demands a proper, correct, intelligible performance. The same applies to the prayers and hymns of the liturgy. All of these things make their inherent capacity to preach effectual only if those present can understand them and so become genuine "hearers". For example, the supremely important Eucharistic Prayer cannot fulfil its preaching function if it is adorned or covered up by other prayers or hymns.

Language does indeed present a tough problem

with regard to this preaching character. It was easy
for the early Church in this respect, for the whole of
public worship in its form and language could be
understood by all the faithful and so was a witness to
the faith. But even if in its present form the liturgy
has, in places, lost its original simplicity and so is not
immediately clear in meaning, and if the strangeness
of the language presents an additional difficulty for
the liturgy as preaching, nevertheless these circumstances do not constitute an insuperable obstacle in
the way of preaching. Whoever faces these facts, and
is not afraid to draw the practical conclusions arising
from them, will find many modes of realization. For
example the office of reader and of prayer-leader take
on fresh importance.

A good and correct form is specially obligatory for
the reading of the lessons at Mass; for the purpose of
these lessons is nothing if not to preach the Word of
God to the congregation. Thus it is most welcome to
see that today it is taken for granted that at all
Sunday Masses, not only the Gospel but also the
Epistle is read aloud. Where this is not done, part of
the Word of God is being withheld from the people,
a part which the liturgy provides for the very
purpose of its being proclaimed. Nor should the quite
unpraiseworthy practice of not reading the lessons
in the vernacular at week-day Masses be accepted as
an inviolable tradition. Serious thought should be
given, rather, as to how we could hear the Word of
God more frequently even on week-days, it might be,
for example, on special feast-days, or in Masses for

youth, or at nuptial Masses, or requiem Masses, or on other occasions. This is only to state the minimum demands. The ultimate goal, however, already realized indeed in many institutions, religious communities, and even some parish churches, is regular, daily preaching. Obviously such considerations provoke many questions that cannot be discussed in detail. For example, the question about who will read, where and how he will read, is not immaterial but of great moment for the task of preaching. How these problems are solved will depend upon the extent to which the lessons actually can be made effective as preaching.

There are certain laws and rules which apply not only to reading aloud, but also to the manner of listening. These must be observed if reading aloud is to achieve its purpose. The faithful, especially the children and youngsters, must be educated in genuine listening. Proper listening is not all that easy and may not be lightly taken for granted. Like so much else in worship it has to be learned. It can only be practised by a man who is not only outwardly but also inwardly at rest, who is capable of recollection, and ready to hear. The fact that some of the faithful are reading the text in their missals as it is read out is all too plainly a sign of how little they know how to listen. They are readers, not hearers of the word. For them no proclamation of the Word is needed. On this point liturgical education means instructing the young – and adults – that the only sensible attitude during proclamation of the Word is that of *listening.* All consider it unseemly if someone reads his prayer-book during the sermon. How much more does this apply when it is the Word of God himself that is being read out.

There is a tremendous power of preaching inherent in the liturgy itself. This power is often restricted and overlaid by inadequate forms. In missionary regions today astounding discoveries are being made of the often unused possibilities for advancing the faith through a properly ordered and intelligible form of public worship.[3] Not only in mission territory, but at home as well the Christian faith has many salutary discoveries to make in this respect, and many pressing problems to solve.

Preaching about public worship

The Church's preaching must impart the undiminished Word of God; hence the working of God in the liturgy is part of its subject-matter, for the Word of God bears witness to the fulness of God's redemptive activity in the past, the present, and the future. The chosen place of this activity in the present is the sacraments. Preaching must therefore speak of them. If this speaking about the sacraments is to be true preaching then it must primarily be a description of the divine redemptive process in them. It dare not content itself merely with exhortation to receive the sacraments frequently and worthily. Also, the aware-

[3] Cf. for example, Hofinger-Kellner: *Liturgy and the Missions*, London, 1957.

ness must be constantly kept alive that it is the risen
Lord himself who imparts salvation to men in all of
the sacraments. The demand and exhortation to
respect and receive the sacrament is then based upon
this preaching of salvation. The sermon and the
instruction on the sacraments ought not to be
regarded as a peripheral topic in preaching. In-
frequent or inadequate preaching on the liturgy
detracts from the glory of God because it does not
fittingly declare God's working through the liturgy.
This too is a contributory cause of the neglect of the
sacraments such as Penance and Anointing of the
Sick by many of the faithful.

At the centre of the whole liturgy stands the
Eucharist. This, then, provides the chief topic for
preaching and instruction on the liturgy. Instruction
on the Mass can take many forms.[4] We might, for
example, speak about the aspects of the Mass, that
is about the Mass as Eucharist, as sacrifice, as a meal,
as a memorial, as an assembly, as the work of Christ
and the congregation, as a meeting with God, and so
on. Special attention is merited by an exposition of
the acclamations and of those prayers and hymns in
which the congregation join. Thus the Dominus
vobiscum, the Oremus, and the Amen must be explained. No less necessary is an exposition of the
Kyrie, Gloria, Credo, Sanctus, and Agnus Dei. Today

---

[4] A wealth of literature has sprung up on this problem. Let us
refer at least to the symposium edited by F. X. Arnold and
B. Fischer: *Die Messe in der Glaubensverkündigung* (Freiburg[2]
1953), which deals with the fundamental questions, historically,
systematically, and practically.

all of these parts of the Mass are said or sung by the congregation. It is therefore more urgent than it was formerly to introduce the children to the meaning of these texts. They must be shown the full depth and richness of these texts, and be made to realize what a dignity for themselves is implied by their use of these prayers and songs.

If the whole liturgy is subject-matter for preaching, then we must also speak of that part which is dealt with in preaching in a particularly niggardly way. When in a sermon or in catechetical instruction one touches on the sacramentals, one enters land as a rule quite strange to the faithful. Perhaps nowhere in the life of devotion does one find so many hazy, even magical and superstitious notions as here. It is strange that the preacher, so often intent on finding *practical* preaching, often neglects this field. Even in religious instruction the young learn very little about this. And yet the faithful come up against sacramentals every day. They use holy water, blessed rosaries, medals, religious pictures and the crucifix. They have their houses, steadings, cars and so on, blessed. It is common experience that not only children, but adults, too, are most interested to hear some clear, reasonable explanation of these things that they receive or do, or hear. On page 121 ff. we have given two examples illustrating what is meant by such explanations.

The doctrine of the sacraments in the new German Catechism is of supreme help to liturgical education. In earlier chapters of this book plenty has been said about that.

The Mass as source of preaching

All the texts of the Mass, the fixed as well as the variable, may serve as sources for preaching. We are speaking of these now not as sources for liturgical instruction but as sources for preaching the faith in general. The value of these texts varies, admittedly. The texts of the Mass are in part texts from holy Scripture, in part prayers composed and prescribed by the Church itself. Obviously these texts cannot claim the same rank as the words of Scripture. But because they declare the Church's faith they supply valuable help to the preacher. Sad to say, they are rarely used thus either in sermons or in catechetical instruction. And yet hidden in the prayers of the Mass lies a rich and almost inexhaustible treasure for preaching. The same is true of the Proper chants of the Mass, the Introit, the Gradual, the Offertory, and Communion. In a special degree these are sources for preaching because they consist predominantly of words from Scripture.

The lessons more than any other part of the Mass can claim to be sources for preaching. There are no fixed rules about this; but the exhortation to take these lessons as the prime subject-matter in preaching the faith has been repeatedly stressed by the leaders of the Church. In this way, arbitrary choice in preaching material is avoided. The preacher is to feel himself bound by the set Word of God. Without making a law out of it, it ought to be the rule that the lessons be chosen as the subject-matter of preaching.

It is well known that the epistles are seldom regularly expounded in the sermon or in religious instruction. The reason usually given is that they are too difficult for the people, particularly for the young, to understand. The obvious answer to that is: all the more is an explanation necessary. Throughout two thousand years the Church has not been afraid to place these texts before the faithful. Therefore the Church thought and still thinks that these texts from the Word of God are there for the people to hear. It is true that in places they are more difficult to understand than the lessons from the gospels. Ought the conclusion not therefore to be that they need to be explained all the more thoroughly and frequently? The lessons from the gospels are felt to be easier because they recount the actions of Christ as concrete parables. The understanding of these is, however, by no means easy: sometimes it is very difficult. The impression that they are apparently simple and easy to grasp may result from the fact that people rest content with superficial and hasty expositions. The interpretation of the parables of Jesus in catechetical handbooks provides numerous examples of this. The deep and true meaning is revealed only to a searching and penetrating enquiry. The lessons from the epistles – usually taken from the letters of St. Paul – present fewer incidents and fewer parables. It is not true to say, however, that they are often abstract and hence difficult to understand. The apostle uses concrete language. It is the language of the pastor, not of the philosopher or theologian. It is true that the line of thought is not always immediately apparent. But these lessons on the whole represent a side of Christian preaching that forms a valuable and helpful complement to the pericopes of the gospels. They arose out of the circumstances of Christian congregations and deal with the foundation and realization in this world of the Christian life of the individual and the Church. Thus they are specially suited for preaching to our congregations. The preacher's function is to declare the word that was spoken or written in those days to his present audience so that it becomes the Word of God for them now, a Word of demand and of grace, of salvation and of judgment.

When we think in this way of the greatness and urgency of preaching, we are brought face to face with a fact that is becoming increasingly a problem. It is common practice to read the notices on Sunday between the reading of the Gospel and the sermon. As we know, these include the announcement of the times of services during the coming week, Masses, devotions, weddings, funerals, etc., and of meetings of organizations and other parochial events. We might ask if this very important place in the Mass, between Gospel reading and Gospel preaching, is the most suitable place for these announcements. By interpolating them here the connection between the read and the preached Word is broken. This interruption has a particularly baneful effect if the notices are very long and varied. The least we can demand on this point is that the notices be shortened as much as possible. Most of the notices could be advertised in the church magazine or on the notice-board. More radically: we might ask if there is not a more appropriate place for these notices. Tradition suggests various possibilities. Today we meet with two principal attempts at a solution. The announcements are made either before or towards the end of Mass. In the first case the opportunity is given to refer to the celebration about to take place. To have the announcements at the end is perhaps the more rational place because they deal with coming events. Both ways require to be tested for a long time yet.

The meaning of the Christian Year[5]

One of the most popular modern conceptions of the Christian year is that it is a tangible representation of the dogmatic and moral truths of Christianity. These truths – so it is argued – are too difficult for simple folk, because they are sublime and abstract. In the feasts of the Christian Year, however, they become tangible, comprehensible, experienced. In the ceremonies, the prayers, and the hymns, they perceive these truths, as it were, with the senses, with their eyes and ears. On this view the Christian Year is a massive form of popular instruction, a popular presentation of the faith. There is much that is justified in this view, but it overlooks the essential nature of the Christian Year.

[5] Cf. *Const.*, arts. 102-11.

There is another way of looking at the Christian Year that is related to this. The Christian Year is seen as a chronological presentation of the life of Christ. The past historical life of Jesus is made present to the faithful through the seasons and the feasts of the Christian Year. On this view the Christian Year is a collection of memorial feasts. Thus in Advent we commemorate the era before Christ; at Christmas, his birth; at Easter, his passion and resurrection; and so on. This interpretation is not utterly false either. It contains a viewpoint that is relatively correct; but the real depth of the Christian Year does not come to light through this view either.

What is the essence of the Christian Year? The essence of the Christian Year lies in making present Christ's redemptive activity through liturgical celebrations. By this we mean not just a conscious making present to one's own mind, but primarily an objective, real re-presentation. We are not interested in memorial feasts wherein some event or other from past history is recalled to mind, but in celebrations wherein that which is commemorated is objectively present. In the feasts of the Church it is not the historical aspect of Christ's life that is made present. There is no repetition of that which happened once upon a time in history. At Christmas Christ is not born again, and at Easter he does not rise again. Without letting ourselves become embroiled in the welter of unresolved theological questions touching on this point, let us be content with the general affirmation that it is not the historical Jesus, but the supra-temporal, divine effect in the redemptive acts that finds re-presentation in the liturgy. Hence it is the person and the redemptive work of Christ that become present in the worship of the Church – really and objectively present what is more, quite independent of human subjective awareness.

In every celebration of the Eucharist, Christ makes his sacrifice, the centre of his redemptive work, present. What is the point, then, of the Christian Year? The Christian Year, the core of which is the daily celebration of the Mass, unfolds the fulness of the mystery of Christ. Each individual feast and season sets out one particular aspect of this mystery, and makes it the special subject of the celebration. Thus in Advent and at Christmas the coming of the Lord is celebrated; at Easter, his death and resurrection.

In terms of this essential interpretation, the different descriptions of the Christian Year should be understood. The Christian Year is popularly called the Year of the Lord. This does not allude to the common idea that every particular year is A.D. something or other. The Lord of whom we speak is Christ. The term "Year of the Lord" expresses the Christian faith that in every liturgical celebration of the year Christ is the living heart. This Christocentric understanding is the basis for two other expressions. We speak of the Year of Grace, because in the yearly cycle of feasts, the redemption which God by his grace has established in Christ is made present. Even the term "Church's Year" ought not to be understood in the superficial sense, as though this were merely a collective name for all the feasts prescribed by the Church in the course of a year. It is true that common parlance betrays this idea. But just as the meaning of the term "Year of the Lord" is not exhausted by the idea that years are numbered from the birth of Christ, nor the term "Year of Grace" by the fact that the incarnation of the Son of God inaugurated a new era of grace, so it is with the term "Church's Year". The Church's Year is the form in which the Church celebrates its worship in the course of a year. In this worship the Church realizes itself and portrays itself. Hence the yearly cycle of liturgical feasts forms "the Church's Year".

Preaching in the setting of the Christian Year

The lessons from holy Scripture that are read out during public worship are linked with the Christian Year. The connection certainly varies in kind and in degree. It is particularly plain in the central seasons of Advent, Lent, and Easter. Then the Church presents the Word of God within the framework of the Christian Year. This Word is itself an integral part of the content of the various feasts, and plays its part in making present the redemptive event. From the close connection between the Christian Year and the Word of God a few rules emerge for the preaching of the faith. There is a fundamental demand that, as a rule, preaching should follow the

Christian Year. The nature and meaning of the
Christian Year justify such a demand; for, as we saw,
the Christian Year is not a collection of just any
devotional forms, but the ordering of the official
public worship which the Church celebrates in the
course of the year. Within this order the Word of
God, too, is presented in the liturgy. Consequently it
should be the rule that preaching, which is the
expounding and living application of the Word of
God, conforms to the order of the Christian Year.
We must, however, guard against making this rule
into a dead principle. That which is good as a rule
need not be necessary every time. There are legitimate reasons – particular occasions in the life of the
congregation, the need to deal with a specific topic,
etc. – that might move the preacher to depart from
this rule. This rule would seem to encounter special
difficulties in catechetical instruction. There, instruction in the faith is commonly given as systematic
catechetical or biblical instruction. Both of these
proceed according to rules that are unaffected by the
Christian Year. Undoubtedly systematic instruction
in the faith is valuable and necessary. But it need not
have the result that we pay no heed to the making
present of the Word of God in public worship. As far
as possible systematic instruction should be accom-
modated to the Christian Year. It is the business
primarily of those who draw up schemes of work to
pay attention to this. To prepare the young for public
worship, especially to explain the meaning and value
of the liturgies of the Sundays and great feast days,

ought not to become dependent upon these possibilities of accommodation. This would have to be a set part of catechetical instruction.

There is another rule concerning preaching linked with the Christian Year. Preaching must explain the true meaning of the feasts and seasons of the Christian Year.

What do we mean by preaching being linked with the Christian Year? This does not mean that one takes up any text from the Mass of the day or from the Divine Office and turns it into the starting-point for an instruction that is in line with neither its biblical origin nor with its liturgical context. Preaching should teach, rather, what is the true content and meaning of the feast. It would seem to be difficult to follow this advice. As experience shows, it is not so plain and straightforward as one might imagine; for both the practice of preaching in sermon and in catechesis, and the literature on the subject, are constantly revealing how strong and tempting is the inclination to *invent* ideas about a feast or season, that do not correspond to its true meaning at all.[6] If the preacher or the teacher wants to teach the undistorted meaning of the Christian Year to his

[6] Informative on this topic is the book of Bruno Dreher: *Die Osterpredigt von der Reformation bis zur Gegenwart* (Freiburg 1951). It provides a historical examination of the Easter sermon, and demonstrates that for centuries the sermon on the greatest feast of the Christian faith has overlooked the central mysteries and been satisfied with peripheral or even secular ideas (in the Baroque period and the Enlightenment respectively).

congregation or pupils, it is absolutely imperative that he himself should first of all be sure of its true and full meaning. It may be objected that this statement is obvious or a platitude. Maybe so, but it has to be made just the same. If a man would preach the Advent message of the Church, he must first experience it himself. How historical, that is how much a record of past events, is much of the preaching of Advent in church and school! And yet it contains faith's whole hope in the world to come. And what sentimentality and childishness do we permit ourselves at Christmas, although the liturgical texts are one solid contradiction of this. There is only one remedy for this and similar misinterpretations: one must make the effort to find the true, objective meaning of the liturgy, using the right kind of expository literature. In this effort we must allow ourselves to be motivated solely by an interest in finding out exactly what the Church wants to preach through the day or the season in question.[7]

---

[7] Not every book or periodical on the Christian Year will give such assistance. Still unsurpassed are the articles on the Christian Year by Joh. Pink, published under various titles in the period 1932-7 in the journal, *Liturgisches Leben*, edited by himself. (Since 1933 the journal has been called *Liturgische Zeitschrift*.) In these articles the author is controlled by the thought that he will only explain the relevant message of the liturgy by what he finds in the text. These studies are of great practical value in the preparation of sermons and instruction, because he links with the meaning discovered, discussions of what this means for the Christian today. In this way the author has studied the principal feasts and seasons as well as the Sundays after Pentecost, the importance of which is so often underestimated.

The third rule for liturgical preaching can be formulated thus: the central festivals of the Christian Year must be regarded according to their rank. There is a gradation of rank and of value among feast days. Even if we accept the fact that all in the liturgy of the Christian Year is of value and must be explained and taught, still, the meaning of the principal seasons must be specially stressed. The seasons to be specially stressed in this way are Christmas (i.e. Advent, Christmas, Epiphany with the Sundays following) and Easter-tide (i.e. Lent, Easter, and the fifty days until Pentecost). We draw special attention to the Sundays between Pentecost and Advent, the so-called "Sundays throughout the year". Their importance is easily overlooked. It is not the feasts which are the oldest part of the Christian Year. Although no feast other than Easter Sunday was celebrated in early Christian times, the first day of every week was celebrated as the day of the resurrection of the Lord. This is still the meaning of Sunday.

The importance of preaching according to the Christian Year

What is the importance of the preaching of the faith being attached to the Christian Year, and carried out in its spirit? Such a connection has far-reaching results both for the substance and for the form of preaching. In the first place such preaching establishes the unity between the liturgical celebration and preaching. We admit that preaching or instructing unconnected to the Christian Year is still possible and legitimate. And yet it is out of place when at worship the preaching and the ceremonies that are performed in the same physical place are in different spiritual areas; when the prayers, lessons, and hymns make up a world that is separate from the world constructed by the preacher. The ideal solution is reached when the mystery of the feast, the words of the liturgy, and the sermon form a unity. In the sphere of religious instruction, too, a disregard of the Christian Year is unwise. Apart from other consequences, the dangerous fact that in the religious mentality of the young a cleavage is thereby created that weakens the contact of his life with the Church, is something that ought to disturb us.

Association with the liturgy of the Christian Year necessarily brings preaching within the atmosphere of the history of redemption. Thus it is in accord with the mode in which the Word of God was revealed. For history is the place where God's redemptive work is revealed. The divine speech and action has, therefore, a history. This is called "the history of redemption". The Christian Year is full of this history, of its incidents, its personalities, and its pattern throughout Old and New Testaments. For anyone who lives in the Christian Year, steeping himself in its spirit and drinking from it, the preaching of that Year will inevitably become a witness to the history of redemption. Then it is no pale, dreary, abstract doctrine about God, but a witness to God's deeds in history, speech filled with life.

Such a style of preaching in terms of the history of redemption is the only preaching that corresponds to the revelation of God. Moreover, it is immeasurably more effective than preaching that ignores the history of redemption. Because here the divine doctrine is presented as an incarnate Word that has entered into human history, it is grasped by the hearer, who is himself a being living, thinking, and acting in history. To man existing in history, a preaching which draws upon historical life appears more credible than a non-historical doctrine that is removed from life. He is more readily convinced by it and is more willing to accept it.

We need have no fear that instruction in the faith in terms of the Christian Year will become monotonous. The opposite is true. Every feast contains a hidden wealth of aspects of divine truth. We need only take a glance at the fathers of the Church to see that they knew how to preach at Easter. Although they did this year in, year out, often giving daily addresses during Easter week, their sermons are never monotonous. They always flow with spiritual depth, because they were in living contact with the history of redemption, and had their source in liturgical action.

It is true that in the liturgy we do not find the whole text of Scripture; but it presents such a wealth of Scripture that it bears witness to the whole faith. As a result, whoever follows the Christian Year will be protected against seeing and teaching only bits of the faith. Year by year the whole history of salvation from the creation of the world, through the Fall and the redemption, until the "restitution of all things" (Acts 3:21) will be brought before his mind. In this the whole world of faith will be unfolded: the truth of God the creator, redeemer, perfecter; the truth about man's true condition, about his destruction and his redemption; the truth about the Church and the world; in short – all the truths of faith. And so the Christian faith helps the one who teaches to make his preaching what it ought to be: a witness to the whole faith.

XIII

WORSHIP AND THE WORLD

THE Eucharist ends with the words: "Ite missa est" – "Go, it is the dismissal." With these words the assembly for public worship is dismissed. Liturgical celebration is not the whole, but only a part of the life of faith. Although of paramount importance, to outward appearance it forms but a small part of Christian life. The importance of the liturgy must be guarded against two one-sided views. Worship is neither an affair on the fringe of the Christian life, nor is it so important that, by comparison, life in the world is meaningless. Celebrating the liturgy and life in the world are not two separate or even mutually exclusive entities. They are two very different but related parts of an all-embracing whole. Having considered the unique significance of the liturgy under numerous aspects, it now remains in conclusion – so that any one-sided interpretation of the liturgy be avoided – to explain the connection between worship and the world.

The distinctive statement of the Christian faith on the relationship of God to the world is thus formulated in the well-known text from St. John's gospel (John 3:16): "For God so loved the world, as to give his only begotten Son; that whosoever believeth in him may not perish, but may have life everlasting." The Christian's faith in the love of God is not the expression of an innocuous or superficial view of the world, that is aware only of the bright and not the dark side of life. Rather, it is the certainty, gained from God's self-revelation, that God will save this world, his own creation, from the destruction brought upon it through man's guilt, and bring it to perfection. Because this faith in the love of God is not the fruit of the direct experience of life, neither is it shattered by such experience. This love of God has become visible in Jesus Christ: "By this hath the charity of God appeared towards us, because God hath sent his only begotten Son into the world, that we may live by him" (I John 4:9). The Church, the society of those who believe in Christ, that owes its existence to this love, has to declare this love of God to the world. The public worship of the Church is the chosen place where this love becomes present through the word and the sacramental sign. The love of God is the deepest mystery and the inner kernel of worship. Its coming to the assembled faithful is the most important event in worship. But the love of God, revealed in Christ, is directed not merely to the assembly of the faithful, but to all mankind. It knows no political, social, cultural, or confessional boundaries, for its goal is the redemption of all. To this love, all men owe their existence, and in it alone do they find eternal fulfilment of their being. And this creative, divine power of love does not stop at the limits of the human race. The whole world in every mode of being owes its existence to this power. Hence in terms of its origin, the world is God's property. Its disorder and malady is not rooted in God's creative act, but in the autocratic turning away from God of the creature endowed with free-will. The power of the love of God intends to make this world, distorted and wounded by sin, once more the property of God, an eternally whole world, a new heaven and a new earth (Apoc. 21:1). And so the infinite love of God embraces the whole world. Thus it embraces both worship and world. In the light of that love, worship and world are not two unrelated entities. Each, although different in nature and function, belongs to the single world of God. The Christian faith sees the deepest reason for their unity and inter-relationship in the universal divine love. This love is not a sentimental feeling, but the ultimate power of God who holds sway over the whole universe. In this world-embracing love of God, the believer sees the unity of the whole of reality. This vision prevents the believing mind from splitting the world into a sacred-liturgical and a profane department. It embraces all as one great province under God's rule, which is the power and love of the creator and Father.

The only valid response a man can make to the love of God is that of love to God, arising from faith. Because God's love meets man principally in worship, it is in worship also that man must realize his love in a special way. Love of God should be the motive power in taking part in public worship. In this frame of mind the Word of God should be heard, the prayers spoken, and the ceremonies performed. The degree of this love determines the value of participation. There is no substitute for it. No painstakingly exact fulfilment of the prescribed ceremonies, no wonderful solemnity can take its place. On the other hand it is not opposed to dignity of form and the effort to achieve a perfect outward expression. On the contrary the attempt to produce an intelligent, worthy, and beautiful form is a sign of the sincerity and seriousness of this love. Liturgical education must teach the faithful to take small and great matter of form seriously, out of love for God, because this is the pathway of the love of God to man, and of man's love to God.

Religious love is also the essential power which the believer exercises in the world. As the believer knows that God's love is present in his whole life, so he understands love of God as the central thought which should determine his behaviour in every situation. Whether it concerns his co-existence with his fellow men, or his mastery of his job, or anything at all that he does, the love born of faith ought always to be his sustaining and normative power.

Thus a second aspect of the unity of Christian life is achieved. Not only the love which comes down from above, but also that which arises from earth in response, embraces the whole of life. Not only God's action, but the action of the believing man also creates the unity of life. No matter how unassailable the pre-eminence of worship is, yet it is but a part of Christian life, which in the full breadth of its realization is a single activity arising from the depths of religious love. In this respect, too, therefore, there is an ultimate unity of liturgy and world.

There is yet another aspect that establishes and assures this unity. The behaviour of God to man is the model of the relationship of the believer to his fellow men. Because God loves our fellow men, so the believer too must love his fellow men. Because God's love knows no bounds, so the believer must love without limit. He must be prepared to realize neighbourly love without reserve to every human being. He is expressly commanded by God to do this. Because the love of God is no sentimental attitude, love of one's neighbour does not demand that we have good feelings towards others. The unpleasant neighbour remains unpleasant, and the burden of putting up with him remains. The political opponent remains in practice, an opponent. But both suffering the unpleasant neighbour, and fighting the opponent are to be done in love. This consists in desiring good to every man, treating him justly, helping him in any distress, and being solicitous for his salvation, for the love of God. Again we must point out that such love must be practised in a special way in public worship. Praying with one another and for one another should be an expression of love. Even in such small things as consideration for others in occupying seats, or when going up to receive Communion, this disposition must be at work. It is the essential nature of intercession that it arises from a loving care of others. Whoever prays for another, cares for him and makes an effort to help him. The quintessence of this care shows itself in a love that does not turn away from any need. Thus, loving solicitude extends far beyond the circle of our fellow worshippers and believers and reaches every man. Like the love of the Father, so is the Son's love, universal: "Love your enemies; . . . and pray for them that persecute . . . you; that you may be the children of your Father who is in heaven, who maketh his sun to rise upon the good and bad and raineth upon the just and unjust" (Matt. 5:44-5). In this way the commandment directs the love of the faithful to the world. By it he is forbidden to indulge in the self-righteous exclusiveness that would account only his own co-religionists of any value. The apostolic admonition (Gal. 6:10): "let us work good to all men, but especially to those who are of the household of the faith", emphasizes the pre-eminence of the Christian society, but at the same time directs our vision to the universal brotherhood of all mankind. The command to love one's neighbour is to be fulfilled towards every man, whatever his political party, whatever his social class, whatever his race, whatever his religion. Like the love of God, love between men creates a unity of existence in the Church and in the world. It forbids the esoteric exclusiveness of a liturgical or religious confederacy, and demands the public and honest affirmation of every man.

As we saw, the love of God is directed not only upon men, but upon the whole of creation. As a result, neither ought the believer to suspend the movement of his love to the world before it reaches the rest of creatures. Here again the divine love is the model for human love. Like God, man, too, should love everything that exists. Because faith regards and loves the things of the world as God's creatures, these have been placed at the service of the liturgy. In the building and furniture of churches, in the liturgical vestments and vessels used in performing the sacraments, the creation appears in the Church's worship. In this way material things are dignified by being used as mediators of the grace of God and expressions of man's piety. How then could the faithful despise or even hate these things? What he has learned to prize in the liturgy, he must respect and love in the world also. The same disposition must rule him as he works in the world. Whether he works with animals, plants, or other things in nature, whether he be occupied in cultural pursuits, in technical, political, or social work, all he does must be done with a positive attitude that is inspired by faith.

It must be admitted that an objection has to be made to this positive evaluation of the world. Does this view not ignore the "wicked world", the reality and power of which is known to faith? Is it not also a one-sided, optimistic interpretation of the life of the faithful in this world? We have already met the same question in our discussion of the love of God for the world. What was said there applies here also. It is undeniable, and recognizable even without faith, that there is a power of evil in the world. But the boundary between the wicked and the good world does not coincide with the dividing line between liturgy and the profane world, between liturgical activity and secular activity. Nor is the line drawn between believers and unbelievers. It is true that the believer has been delivered by God from the power of evil, and that the grace of God supports him in his fight against evil. But because, after justification, he still retains his freedom of decision, he can still surrender to the enemies of God. And so the boundary between the good and the wicked world runs right through the being of every individual man. The believer who comes to worship does not leave the wicked world at the church door, neither, on the other hand, does he enter it simply by stepping out of church. Within worship there can be both the good and the wicked world. The power of evil – absurd as this sounds – can exist within the Church. It exists there in so far as men give it space. And as worship, so also the world has to be seen dialectically. It is not the *wicked* world purely and simply. In it, too, we find both the power of good and the power of evil. But as God does not love evil, yet loves this world in spite of the evil in it, and as his love aims at liberating this world from the destructive power of evil, so and not otherwise is the love of the Christian directed to this world. The Christian does not shut his eyes to the evil in the world. At the same time he knows how to distinguish between the evil that is in man and that expresses itself in his deeds, and evil in super-human spheres. The believer respects and loves the reality of the world because he knows that it is God's creation, which is to be protected from the destructive power of evil, and upon which shines the glory of restoration to eternal perfection.

This last way of looking at the subject makes it plain, therefore, that it is not a question of tearing worship and world apart. Worship bears a relation to the world, and the world is integrated in worship. The very purpose of worship is to make the faithful able to live properly in the world. The whole of a Christian's earthly life is enclosed in a single great bond. In this way liturgical piety broadens out to include a properly understood *secular* piety. This is not *worldly* piety, which would indeed be the antithesis to the piety of faith. Secular piety, in contrast, rests upon the love of God which man receives through faith. In essence it is nothing other than the realization of the love towards the world, as God's handiwork, that springs from faith.

This comprehensive view of liturgical piety necessarily precipitates a corresponding understanding of liturgical education. Liturgical education does not make up the whole of Christian education; but it is its kernel, for it contains the ground-plan of the whole. On these terms, liturgical education is orientated towards an education from faith, that is total and applied to the world. If this slant is ignored, then liturgical piety and education become a detached and museum-like province from which radiates no power to master life in the world. In liturgical education lies the foundation of the total education of the man of faith. By total education is meant the formation in the Christian of the proper existence within, and

relationship to, the whole of reality. In such Christian
education, liturgical education reaches fulfilment.